LOVE ALONE IS CREDIBLE

HANS URS VON BALTHASAR

LOVE
ALONE
IS
CREDIBLE

Translated by D. C. Schindler

IGNATIUS PRESS   SAN FRANCISCO

Original German edition:
Glaubhaft ist nur Liebe
© 1963 by Johannes Verlag, Einsiedeln

Cover photograph:
Sacred Heart of Jesus
An image scratched on the wall at Auschwitz
photograph by Wieslaw M. Zieliński
Auschwitz, Poland

Cover design by Roxanne Mei Lum

ISBN 978-0-89870-881-3
Library of Congress Control Number 2003116647
Printed in the United States of America ∞

Quisquis Scripturas divinas
vel quamlibet earum partem
intellexisse sibi videtur, ita ut
in eo intellectu non aedificat
istam geminam caritatem,
nondum intellexit.

— ST. AUGUSTINE

Tout ce qui ne va point à
la charité est figure.
L'unique objet de l'Ecriture
est la charité.

— PASCAL

Contents

Preface

What is specifically Christian about Christianity? Never in the history of the Church have Christian thinkers thought it ultimately adequate to answer this question by pointing to a series of mysteries one is required to believe; instead, they have always aimed at a point of unity that would serve to provide a justification for the demand for faith. They sought a *logos* that, however particular it might be, nevertheless had the power to persuade, and indeed to overwhelm, a *logos* that, in breaking out of the sphere of "accidental historical truths", would lend these truths a necessity. Miracles and fulfilled prophecies may have their role to play (a role whose significance seems to have diminished considerably after the biblical criticism of the Enlightenment), but they point to something that lies beyond them. The Patristic Age, the Middle Ages, and the Renaissance, with offshoots that extend into the present age, established the reference point within the realm of the cosmos and world history; after the Enlightenment, the modern age shifted this point to an anthropological center. If the first approach bears the limitations of temporal history, the second also betrays a fundamental flaw,

for neither the world as a whole nor man in particular can provide the measure for what God wishes
to say to man in Christ; God's Word is unconditionally theo-logical, or, better, theo-pragmatic: what
God wishes to say to man is a deed on his behalf,
a deed that interprets itself before man and for his
sake (and only therefore to him and in him).[1] What
we intend to say about this deed in this book is that
it is credible only as love—specifically, as God's own
love, the manifestation of which is the glory of God.

Christian self-understanding (and therefore theology) can be interpreted neither in terms of a wisdom
that surpasses the knowledge of the world's religions
through a divine utterance (*ad majorem gnosim rerum
divinarum*) nor in terms of man's definitive achievement of personal and social fulfillment through revelation and redemption (*ad majorem hominis perfectionem
et progressum generis humani*), but solely in terms of
the self-glorification of divine love: *ad majorem Di-
vini Amoris GLORIAM*. In the Old Testament, this
glory (*kabod*) is the presence of Yahweh's radiant
majesty in his Covenant (and through this Covenant
it is communicated to the rest of the world); in the
New Testament, this sublime glory presents itself as
the love of God that descends "to the end" of the
night of death in Christ. This extremity (the true

[1] On the immanent aspect, see "God Speaks As Man", in *Explorations in Theology*, vol. 1: *The Word Made Flesh* (San Francisco: Ignatius Press, 1989), 69–93.

eschato-logy)—which could never have been anticipated from what we know of the world or man—
can be welcomed and perceived in its truth only as
the "Wholly-Other".

Thus, this sketch will be an elaboration of what I
endeavored in my larger work *The Glory of the Lord*,
that is, it will be a "theological aesthetic" in the
twofold sense of a subjective theory of perception
and a theory of the objective self-interpretation of
the divine glory; it will seek to show that this theological method, far from being a negligible and dispensable by-product of theological thought, cannot
but lay claim to the center of theology as the only
valid approach, while the approaches founded on the
cosmos or world history, on the one hand, or on
anthropology, on the other, can be presented as secondary and complementary at best.

What is here called an "aesthetic" is therefore
characterized as something properly theological,
namely, as the reception, perceived with the eyes of
faith, of the self-interpreting glory of the sovereignly
free love of God. This aesthetic has therefore nothing in common with the philosophical aesthetic that
one finds, for example, in the Christian thought
of the Renaissance (Ficino), or the Enlightenment
(Shaftesbury), or German Idealism (Schelling or
Fries), or the theology of mediation (de Wette),
or even in what Schleiermacher calls aesthetic piety
(*The Christian Faith*, no. 9). At most, a parallel could

be drawn with Scheler's phenomenological method, insofar as this method appeals to a pure self-giving of the object; however, in theology the methodological "bracketing out" of existence falls altogether out of consideration. We cannot strive for a philosophical "disinterestedness" of pure contemplation (*epochē* as *apatheia* for the sake of *gnosis*), but only Christian *in-differencia* as the sole possible methodological disposition for the reception of the "disinterestedness" of divine love, which has no end beyond itself and is thus absolute.

The present sketch intends only to lay out this central methodological point and will leave aside the whole abundance of content that one may find, for example, in other studies such as Victor Warnach's *Agape: Die Liebe als Grundmotiv der neutestamentlichen Theologie* (1951) and C. Spicq's *Agapè dans le Nouveau Testament* (1958–1959), which also contain extensive bibliographies.

It goes without saying that the following essay contains nothing fundamentally new, and that it seeks in particular to stay true to the thought of the great saints of the theological tradition: Augustine, Bernard, Anselm, Ignatius, John of the Cross, Francis de Sales, Thérèse of Lisieux. . . . Lovers are the ones who know most about God; the theologian must listen to them.

The methodological point this essay seeks to develop represents, at the same time, the proper theological *kairos* of our time: if *this* approach does not manage to move our age, it has scarcely any chance left of encountering the heart of Christianity in its unadulterated purity. In this respect, this little book stands as the positive, constructive complement to my earlier book *Razing the Bastions*,[2] which cleared the way for this approach.

Hans Urs von Balthasar
Basel
New Year's Day, 1963

---

[2] Hans Urs von Balthasar, *Razing the Bastions: On the Church in This Age* (San Francisco: Ignatius Press, 1993).

1. The Cosmological Reduction

In order to bring home the credibility of the Christian message to the world, the Church Fathers presented this message against the backdrop of the world religions, whether they viewed these religions in their multiplicity (Eusebius, Arnobius, Lactantius) or whether they also grasped them in their religious and philosophical unity (Justin, Origen, Augustine). Christianity thus stands out against this background as the fulfillment of the fragmented meaning of the world (*logos spermatikos*), which in the Word Made Flesh (*Logos sarx*) achieves its unity and fullness and redeemed freedom (Clement and Athanasius). Against this backdrop, Christianity represented not only a fulfillment, but also a call to conversion, insofar as all of the fragmentary *logoi* absolutized themselves and thus put up a sinful resistance to the true Logos (Augustine in the *Civitas Dei*). The relationship between the Old and New Covenant appeared within this general schema of fulfillment as a particular case,[1] for, here, the prophetic structure of the Old Testament becomes clear in the

---

[1] Without a sharp distinction, however, since the Bible was in fact also read as a synopsis of world history, and not only as the book of the Covenant of Israel.

New Testament fulfillment. The Christian message could thus be made credible, both because it unified what was fragmented and also because it ransomed what was held captive by converting what was perverted. To be sure, this was not as easy within the context of a static conception of the cosmos (as in Dionysius, for whom there remains scarcely any room for Christ within the world's structure), as it was when the cosmos unfolded in a "historical narrative", whether this story is a dualistic drama (Manicheanism) with a happy ending (Valentinus); tells of a kingdom of God or heavenly Jerusalem that has descended into the "region of dissimilarity" and which makes its pilgrimage through the ages, called home by the Bridegroom (Origen, Augustine, in *Confessions*, books 11–13); tells of a nature that proceeds forth and then returns (Eriugena, Thomas, Ficino, Boehme, Schelling); is of a primal matter that is impregnated by the Logos in order to give birth to Sophia (Soloviev); or "evolves" toward the marriage feast of the "Omega day" (Teilhard).

This approach was possible because these Christian thinkers took over the identity between philosophy and theology that had prevailed in the ancient cultures as a self-evident fact. Equally evident to them was the unity of the natural and supernatural orders: God has been manifest from the beginning of the world and from Adam onward, and the pagan world failed to recognize that which is clearly there to be seen (Rom 1:18f.); it had "no excuse" for rejecting obedience to the "eternal power and divinity that has been made known" and was thus punished with humiliating idolatry. In short, the ancient world's unifying principles—the Stoic cosmic Logos, the Neoplatonic hierarchy of being that extends from matter to the superessential One, the abstract majesty of Rome's world-unifying power— are redeemable schematic prefigurations of the personal God-Logos, who has drawn close to the world through the history of Israel, a history that fulfills the cosmos and the various religions [*Ökumene*]. The world was created in this Logos, the true "place of the ideas", and can therefore be understood only in the light of this Logos. Christianity marched triumphantly to Rome and from Rome to the ends of the earth—what more was needed to prove that this fulfillment was not only ideal but also real? "Everything that is good and beautiful belongs to us."[2] If this is the case, then why should the Carolingian Academy under Alcuin, in the same spirit, not claim that ancient philosophy received a special illumination by the Logos and view Socrates as a disciple of Christ? Why not allow oneself, with Boethius, to be consoled as a Christian by philosophy, since Boethius perceives the One Logos in his contemplation of the glory of the cosmos? The ancient

[2] Justin, *Apg.* II, c. 13.

worldview—whether it is understood more in the sense of Plato, Aristotle, the Stoics, or Plotinus and Proclus—is permeated by the divine and contains within an image of God. The world, as the ancients saw it, was sacred and, in a formal sense, lacked nothing but the center. With the establishment of the center, God's *agapē* appeared to fulfill the cosmic powers of love to overflowing. Indeed, according to the Areopagite, God's *agapē* had a rightful claim to the title of the true *eros*, and all the power of *eros* governing creation found its center therein. Because the biblical Sophia inherited all things in the Incarnation, it satisfied the pagan search for wisdom (philo-sophia), and it therefore appropriated for itself the intelligible unity and rationality of this search. The transition that fulfilled the philosophical universe in the Christian-theological one granted to reason, enlightened and strengthened by grace, the highest possible vision of unity. Because of this unity, the question whether revelation introduced a special principle of unity was all but left behind.

It is only from within this perspective that we can make sense of and justify a project like Cusanus' *De pace fidei* (1453), which came at the end of the Middle Ages. In this work, Cusanus extends his hand, over the centuries, to Boethius, Dionysius, and Alcuin. When Christ, the cosmic Logos, can no longer bear his vexation with the plurality of religions on earth, he summons a heavenly council, assembling all the leaders of the various confessions. These confessions discover their inner unity through conversation with the Logos and with Peter, his representative. "You do not find a different faith" in the various wisdom teachings, Christ explains, "but rather one and the same faith lies behind each one. For . . . there can be only a single Wisdom", which is the original enfolding (*complicatio*) of all of the partial wisdoms. All the different forms of pantheism presuppose the unity of divinity; in every genuine belief in creation, one can find the doctrine of the Trinity; the Incarnation stands above every genuine prophetic religion as its fulfillment; and so forth. But such a consensus is possible only insofar as each religion acknowledges that, behind them all, stands the God who is Wholly-Other and Ever-Greater: "God as Creator is the Threefold and the One; as infinite, he is neither the Threefold nor the One, nor anything that can be uttered in speech. For the names that we attribute to God are drawn from creatures, while he himself, considered in himself, is unutterable and exalted above all things that can be named or expressed." The plurality of religions, Cusanus concludes, is due primarily to the simplicity of the uneducated; it lies more in the rites than in the reality to which these rites point. The wise men of each religion should have no difficulty coming together at that spiritual place wherein all the fragments of wisdom find their center in a catholic unity.[3]

---

[3] *Opera omnia* (Meiner, 1959), 7:7, 11, 16, 20, 62.

The Renaissance seems to represent a recurrent triumph of the same approach. In laying down the golden foundations of the ancient world's humanistic wisdom tradition once again behind the hairsplitting of the Medieval schools and the abuses of the monasteries, which had lost them their credibility, the Renaissance thinkers thought they were giving Christianity back its center and therefore its inner catholicity—and therefore also its credibility. Dante took the first auspicious steps, and, behind the scholastic Augustine, Petrarch had once again rediscovered the existential Augustine of the *Confessions*, who sought a religion that would bring Platonism to completion. Augustine's early writing *De vera religione* can be seen as the model for all of the theology of the Renaissance. "Precisely because we are Christians," Petrarch wrote to Giovanni Colonna, "philosophy must become for us nothing but the love of wisdom; God's wisdom, however, is his logos—it is Christ; and thus we must love him in order to become true philosophers."[4] Even monasticism recovered its credibility through Petrarch and the Humanists, because they understood it and lived it as the universal human form of the contemplative life;

[4] *Ep. Famil.* 4:4. For an account of the history leading up to this, see Jean Leclercq's *The Love of Learning and the Desire for God*, trans. Catharine Misrahi (New York: Fordham University Press, 1982), and also his article "Etudes sur la vocabulaire monastique du Moyen-âge," in *Studia Anselmiana*, 48 (Rome, 1961).

from Raymond Llull the way leads to the editor of his *Contemplationes*, Lefèvre d'Etaples; the veneration of every pure, religious logos of humanity (Erasmus' philo-logy) becomes the golden background illuminating the adoration of the divine word; ever deeper reflections of the biblical wisdom are discovered in the ancient wisdom, and vice versa. We see this, for example, in Ficino's *Concordantia Mosis et Plationis*, in which Plato provides the rational explication of the New Testament, while being in turn dependent on the Old Testament. Humanism and the religion of the Bible exerted a reciprocal influence on one another in the fifteenth and sixteenth centuries,[5] as it once did in the renaissance of the twelfth century.[6]

But the return to the pure Logos, which was for the Humanists simultaneous with the call back to the pure words of the Bible, also brought about the Reformation. Renouncing all dependence on philosophy for the first time, the Reformation allowed God's evangelical Word and the Christian faith to encounter one another in a naked and unguarded way. So naked, indeed, that the question of the Word's "credibility" was dismissed as a concern to provide a justification, already on human reason's terms, for the pure obedience of pure faith to the pure Word, and thus to water down that obedience.

---

[5] Cf. the works of Renaudet and "Courants religieux et humanisme etc." (Colloque de Strasbourg, 1957) (P.U.F., 1959).

[6] M.-D. Chenu, *La théologie au XII*^{e} *siècle* (Vrin, 1957).

Unfortunately for the Reformation, however, it was increasingly impossible to give an answer to the haunting question of credibility, because of the obstacles presented not only by a concept of faith that had been narrowed through polemics, but also by the position in which the Christian Church found herself as a result of the Western schism. There is nothing that could have made the Christian faith less credible to the incipient modern age than a divided Church: precisely because the support from the philosophical worldview had been abandoned, the main thing that could justify the specific and particular credibility of the Gospel to those outside the faith was obedience to Christ's primary commandment to preserve his peace in unity.[7] The Christian in-fighting of confessional polemics that took

---

[7] In one of his satirical parables, Lessing described how the various inhabitants of a palace were suddenly awoken one night by the call of "Fire!" and each attempted to save what he took to be the dearest of all his possessions: one of various versions of the palace plans, all of which were said to come from a single architect: " 'If we can only save this,' each thought; 'the palace can burn only where it is shown on the plan.' And so each one ran out into the street clutching the plan rather than rushing to aid in saving the palace." They showed one another on the plans where the palace was burning, but none of them was interested in putting out the fire if the place did not appear on his own plan: "Somebody else can put the fire out there, it's none of my business!" (*Theol. Schriften*, 3:95f.).

With the same bitterness, Soloviev recounts a similar parable for the whole of Christianity, comprising both the Eastern and the Western schisms (*Russia and the Universal Church*), *Werke*, Wewel 2 (1954): 184f.

its place forced the question of the theological credibility of Christianity as a whole into second place,
and, seeing these polemics, the world felt compelled
to tread the pre-Reformation path in a much more
rigorous and radical way. There is perhaps nothing
more disturbing in the intellectual history of the
modern age than how imperceptibly the old view
of the world passed over into the new: what was or
appeared to be theology yesterday has turned today
—who can say how?—into philosophy and rational-
ism.

The philosophical worldview of the Renaissance
was a resurrection of the ancient worldview; in other
words, it was religious and mythological. Already in
Dante's time, the intellectual spirits or cosmic powers were called angels or intelligences or "gods", and
even the gods of the *Timaeus* were seen as "created"
by the Demiurge as a gift to the world. One finds
a living and spirit-permeated cosmos present everywhere behind the Christian doctrine of the Incarnation. It was therefore possible to present "religion
in general" once again (as it was in Boethius' *Con-
solatio*) without the educated reader's losing sight of
its connection with the higher Christian synthesis.

Thomas More's *Utopia* (1516) thus stands intellectually quite near to Cusanus' heavenly council,
and for that reason still far from what will later
claim to be a "natural religion", tolerant of all confessional differences. What we see in the religion

of this founder of Utopia is an example of the reduction of Christianity to its luminous fundamental truths, a view that brackets out the distortions
that have sedimented in the history of the Church
and that, with all good intentions, relativizes its accidental "positivities". It is for this reason that, when
Christianity was eventually proclaimed to the Utopians, it "made such an inconceivably powerful impres-
sion", for it "seemed to correspond most closely to
the faith that had the most adherents among them".
The Utopian religion's lack of violence in all things,
and especially in its dissemination, corresponds to
Christ's own attitude; the religion's view of common ownership corresponds to "the common life of
the first apostles, which Christ esteemed so highly";
the Christian relationship to God shines quite clearly
through the Utopians', which was formed through
reverential fear and joyful love, through zealous personal and communal prayer; their living belief in the
afterlife and their view of death; their belief in miracles; their selfless service to their fellow men, which
they undertake "without the slightest concern for
any recompense", and with respect to which "they
are more highly esteemed the more they endeavor
to become the slaves" of their fellow men; their
widespread practice of celibacy and a sort of monasticism; their respect for priests; their custom of reciprocal confession and forgiveness, and their rule
that no one shall bring a sacrifice to the Lord's altar
until he has reconciled himself with his brothers and

been cleansed of all feelings of anger; their habitual awareness of living in dependence on divine grace —this and other features suffice to show that the Utopian religion is a "symbol" for Christianity, just as the Grail had been a symbol in the Middle Ages for the Christian sacramental life. It is only within the framework of this symbolism that the question can arise among the Utopians "whether God himself did not desire the variety of ways of faith, so that each might stimulate the other"; and if, at the end of the discussion, the Utopians confess their willingness before God to accept "a better religion, which is more pleasing to God", if such a thing were to be found, they nevertheless do so once again under a certain condition: "unless God is pleased by the multiplicity of religions".

The Humanistic worldview thus still presented the Christian world-logos, albeit stripped down and distilled to its essence. This was the goal of the proponents of the "third power",[8] and they pointed back to this essence all the more determinedly as their disgust for the destructive fighting within the Church grew. But the Platonism of the Renaissance was itself backward-looking; with respect to the emerging natural sciences, it was already anachronistic. Its "demythologizing" was by the same stroke "humanizing": in imperceptible steps, it replaced the

[8] Friedrich Heer, *Die Dritte Kraft: Der europäische Humanismus zwischen den Fronten des konfessionellen Zeitalters* (Fischer, 1959).

ancient and Christian world-logos with "natural" religion, ethics, and philosophy, as they correspond to the nature common to all peoples and ages. According to its interpretation of Romans 1:18f., one part of the content of revelation was inherited by this natural religion, another part by the "positive" religions—Christianity and others. But these positive religions were being summoned before the judgment seat of mankind with increasing insistence, and with ever greater charges to answer for.

The long-prepared breakthrough occurs with Herbert of Cherbury; severing the knowledge and service of God from their Christian roots, he founds them on a self-sufficient science of religion, which provides the formal principles governing every religion that is, or claims to be, revealed. To be sure, his natural concept of God is saturated with content from the Christian tradition, just as it is in More and in the English freethinkers that came after him; however, he presents this content as something that can be established and justified by pure reason. Because this concept presupposes the ancient and Christian theo-cosmology at every turn (which makes the theo-cosmology in part responsible for it), it is quite difficult to determine to what extent Christianity is being appealed to in justifying the concept. Under the pretense of being a synthesis of philosophy and theology, this hybrid governs the great endeavors of the succeeding age, while the

2. The Anthropological Reduction

Next to the cosmological reduction, another was gradually taking shape, one that displaced the locus of verification from the increasingly demythologized cosmos (which was therefore becoming less of a rival to Christianity) to the human being, who recapitulated the entire world in himself. The ancient and patristic image of man as the "frontier" (*methorion*) between the world and God was resurrected in the Renaissance, with its frequent hymns to man's dignity. Man is God's partner, and their reciprocal conversation ends with God himself becoming man. Not only is man a microcosm, but, in the emerging natural sciences, he is also the one who gives the cosmos its structure, a cosmos he transcends through reason. This is how Kant describes man, as he brings the Enlightenment to its conclusion. But Christianity had already begun to be measured by human nature long before Kant. Pascal did so magnificently in a way that towers over every other attempt of the kind: according to Pascal, man is a monstrous chimera that thwarts all attempts at rational interpretation; he is a creature that can harmonize his irreconcilable proportions, his dialectical intertwining

31

of *grandeur* and *misère*, only by looking at his reflection in the God-man. Herein lies the beginning of the existential apologetic, or the "method of immanence".

The confessional controversies and the disenchantment of the world cooperate to bring about the abrupt turn to a purely human and predominantly ethical religion. Christianity becomes all the more easily understood in light of this religion, insofar as both make universal human claims and both therefore possess an essential inward drive to universality. From Spinoza (*Tractatus theologico-politicus*, 1670), through Mendelssohn, to Bergson (*Two Sources of Morality and Religion*, 1932), liberal Judaism also affirmed a universal human religion that transcended all national borders. From John Locke's *Reasonableness of Christianity* (1695), in which he introduced the "anthropological proof for the existence of God" (spirit can come only from spirit), the pathway leads to John Toland's *Christianity not Mysterious* (1696) and to Matthew Tindal's *Christianity as Old as the Creation* (1730). According to Locke, man has the obligation to measure the revelation he encounters by the yardstick of his reason; in Toland, we find a peeling away of the non-Christian outer husk of pagan mysteries (that is, sacraments and speculative dogma) in order to reach Jesus' simple and universal proclamation; finally, Tindal deliberately secularizes Augustine's *Civitas Dei ab Abel*, turning it into a natural religion that gives honor to God and cultivates the best in man, a religion in which priests have no authority to interfere in the least. For a religion that has been reduced to such dimensions, Christ becomes a teacher of pure truth and an example of pure living, while Paul's notion of the "representative suffering" that justifies sinners becomes inconceivable and a transgression of reason (as Thomas Chubb says explicitly in *The True Gospel,* 1738). Schleiermacher will be the first to attempt the impossible, namely, to reintroduce (Luther's) Paul into an anthropocentric theology.

This reduction culminates in Kant. For him, everything that is humanly knowable in the strict sense is restricted to the synthesis of sensible intuition and concept, while all the ideas that lie beyond this, in "pure reason", prove to be "practical" conditions of possibility of ethical behavior. When I act, I know that I cannot do so except by presupposing the categorical validity of a universal ("catholic") norm, which absolutely transcends me as an empirical subject and which includes the idea of freedom, immortality, and divinity. Here, the unfathomable depths of human nature gape wide, and Kant stands before them in wonder. The more deeply he enters into them, the more unfathomable they become: "There is something in us that can never cease to amaze us once we have set our eyes upon it, and it is precisely this that raises *mankind* conceptually to a dignity that one would never have suspected in *man* as an object of experience. . . . The fact that we *can* do what we quite easily and clearly understand that we *ought* to do, this superiority of the *supersensual man* in us over the *sensual man*, who is *nothing* in comparison with the former (if they were to come into conflict), even though the latter is *everything* in his own eyes: this inalienable moral capacity is an object of supreme wonderment, and it becomes all the more amazing the longer one contemplates this true (and not invented) ideal, so much so that we can forgive those who, misled by the inconceivability of this capacity, which is after all practical, this *supersensual* power in us, take it to be something supernatural. By supernatural, I mean something that does not lie within our own power and does not belong to us, but is rather the influence of another, higher spirit. Nevertheless, they are quite wrong." For Kant, here lies "the solution to the problem of the New Man, and even the Bible seems to have envisioned nothing else"; this is "the teaching of the biblical faith, insofar as it can be deduced from ourselves by means of reason",[1] which is what Kant calls "pure religious faith".

It is here that all of the pathways of the modern age intersect. First, we see in this the transition

---

[1] Kant, *Streit der Fakultäten I: Allgemeine Anmerkung; von Religions sekten* (Prussian ed., 7:58f.).

from Luther to Karl Barth, insofar as Luther had deposed (Aristotelian) reason in order to make room for faith. But in the meantime, the reason that Luther rejected acquired a Cartesian structure; it became scientific, world-constructing reason. By means of his critical method, Kant thus restricted this Promethean power to something under man's control. Being thus limited, reason had nothing more to do with religion and so it became what the young Karl Barth called an "idol factory", and to that extent an adversary of genuine faith. And even when Kant allotted the awe-inspiring realm that stretches out between the empirical man and the idea of mankind to ethics as a space in which to unfold, nevertheless even ethics is nothing more than another human possibility, albeit a practical-existential one. If Christian faith cannot be reduced to one of these two functions, it has to lie beyond both theoretical and practical philosophy. But what if the subject's ethical dimension, as Kant described it, should point to an infinite and absolute subjectivity, and thus what if the religious tension between finite and infinite subjectivity should come to pass as an event in this realm? We would then have to ask: Who or what is this absolute subjectivity? Is it man's own transcendental structure? If it is, then the charges of atheism brought against Fichte were justified, and thus Feuerbach becomes the only logical successor to Kant, insofar as he posits the tension between man and mankind as "the divine".

In order to avoid this outcome, the young Schleiermacher sought a third "faculty" in the subject, beyond the theoretical and practical reason ("metaphysics and morals") that he abandoned to Kant's
judgment, as functions under the control of Promethean man. At first, he called this third faculty "intuition and feeling", in contrast to "thought and action".[2] "All intuition proceeds from the influence of
the intuited object upon the intuiting subject", but
this impulse is the experience or feeling of the totality; what he is speaking of here, in other words, is
a primal and ineffable unity of the two aspects, before they divide into "image" and "feeling".[3] In his
work *The Christian Faith*, he eventually replaces the
first formulation with a second one, namely, the "absolute dependence", which is the most fundamental
experience of creaturehood. But even this is "neither
knowledge nor an act, but rather a determination of
feeling or immediate self-consciousness".[4] Historically speaking, what we see here is no doubt yet
another reference back, beyond the Kantian interpretation of Thomas (and Aristotle), to the Augustin-

[2] Schleiermacher, *Reden über die Religion*, second speech, ed. R.
Otto, 32. [English: *On Religion: Speeches to Its Cultured Despisers*, trans.
Richard Crouter (Cambridge: Cambridge University Press, 1988).]

[3] Ibid., 42, 46–50.

[4] Schleiermacher, *Der christliche Glaube*, 2nd ed. 1830, "Introduction", nos. 3–4. [English: *The Christian Faith*, ed. H. R. Mackintosh
and J. S. Stewart (Edinburgh: T. and T. Clark, 1989).]

ian-Platonic notion of the immediate *"illuminatio"* of the subject by the infinite and all-embracing good. From this perspective, Schleiermacher describes the religious subject as pure passivity (παθεῖν τὰ θεῖα), though this notion has become much more radical than the old concept because of the Lutheran-Kantian (-Barthian) renunciation of all "metaphysics and morals".

Nevertheless, insofar as this primal experience nevertheless claims to be, in its innermost essence, an affection of the pious soul, it remains a human "capacity".[5] As such, it is open to philosophical analysis. On the one hand, in the *Dialektik*, Schleiermacher is able to demonstrate the inner finitude and polarity of all thinking about the infinite, which thus reveals its dependence on the absolute-infinite; on the other hand, through self-analysis and an inquiry into its conditions of possibility, the Christian pious soul, in its historical contingency, can discover its causal origin in the effective impulse of "Jesus of Nazareth". It is this impulse, then, that reunites and reconciles the pious subjectivity with the *universum* (God) out of its fallenness from itself and its consciousness of sin. Everything gets decided by the fact that, in his dogmatic theology, Schleiermacher subsumes Christology under the pious consciousness of redemption as its condition of possibility: dogmatic statements

[5] *Reden* 1:13.

are genuinely scientific only insofar as they relate to this consciousness. In the last analysis, if Christ's historical influence in history is to avoid remaining "purely empirical" and therefore meaningless for dogmatics, we would have to interpret it in terms of the category of the inner historicity of the spirit (Schelling). But in this case, it becomes at best the final completion ("revelation") of the evolving series of the absolute spirit's self-presentation in symbols (in "myth"). Though this was Drey's solution, it was a path that Schleiermacher did not wish to follow.

Schleiermacher's approach, which was inspired by Lutheran pietism, was played out in every conceivable orthodox and liberal variation through the nineteenth and twentieth centuries. It has reappeared in Rudolph Bultmann: what Schleiermacher called feeling, Bultmann calls existence; what Schleiermacher identified as the fallen consciousness of guilt, Bultmann describes as existence in the state of fallenness in the world, in the grips of care and angst; what Schleiermacher called consciousness of reconciliation becomes "detachment from the world" (in the Platonic, the Kantian, or the Johannine sense?). Once again, Bultmann, like Schleiermacher, brings the "process" that occurs as an event in existence into a causal nexus with the proclamation of the reconciling death of Jesus of Nazareth, which reaches us through history. The power of this event lies in the proclamation, and we can ultimately set aside whatever event might actually have occurred in history—indeed, in the last analysis, the actual event is also dispensable in Schleiermacher's dogmatic theology.[6] Historically speaking, there is nothing "to see"; we are simply to lay hold, in faith, of the proclaimed Word that has already laid hold of us. The measure, or the touchstone, of faith remains, even here, human existence. The resurrection of that existence is the most decisive thing, the sole miracle, which makes all others superfluous. As Lessing put it, "Only one who tries to convince people about inconceivable things needs to perform miracles, in order to make what is inconceivable plausible by comparison with other things. But miracles are not necessary for the one who refuses to teach any doctrine that cannot be verified by each person on his own."[7]

Catholic theology, too, eventually thought that it also had to make use of this method of verification, which had become the modern one, and it did so at the end of the nineteenth century in what became

---

[6] In *The Christian Faith*, he develops all of the fundamental propositions under three headings: as affections of the pious subject, as affirmations concerning the state of the cosmos, and as affirmations concerning God. The second and third forms are derived from the first and are "strictly speaking superfluous" (*Sendschreiben an Lücke*, ed. von Mulert [1908], 47f.).

[7] Lessing, *Theolog. Schriften* 1:40.

known as modernism. The central presupposition of modernism, in a nutshell, is that every objective dogmatic proposition must be measured in terms of its suitability to the religious subject, in terms of its positive effects on and capacity to complete and fulfill that subject. To be sure, this fulfillment has to occur within the subject's process of coming to perfection; this process includes deaths and conversions of every degree and kind, which the ever-greater truth demands from the subject in order that it may become capable of embodying the objective proposition. And, of course, in relation to God, we have to understand subjectivity as pure neediness in absolute dependence. Nevertheless, whatever God reveals to this subjectivity in grace must exist in such a way and be expressed in such a way that the subjectivity is able to assimilate it to itself, and thereby to grow. The primary objection that was raised against modernism—namely, that revelation's forms of expression would thus fluctuate with the historical transformations of religious subjectivity—is in fact of less concern than the initial anthropological determination of the criterion for revelation.

The subject's "dynamism" can take a predominantly historical or a predominantly inward, pietistic form; it can also appear as a comprehensive philosophical project—for example, that of Joseph Maréchal or Maurice Blondel—in which man is interpreted as finite spirit. Though this project need not be interpreted ultimately according to modernist thinking, it nevertheless leads to an anthropological justification of revelation. We see this in Blondel, insofar as the acting substratum of his philosophy remains just as abstract (*"le" Vouloir, "l" 'Action*) as it had been in German Idealism (*"der" Geist* in Hegel, *"der" Wille* in Schopenhauer, and *"die" intellektuelle Anschauung* in Schelling). Moreover, in Blondel, this substratum, transcending all finite goals through a restlessly ascending dialectic, reaches the frontier of the Absolute (God), and thus man is compelled to attain fulfillment by transcending himself in the absolute decision.[8] A similar thing occurs in Maréchal: the dynamism of the intellect, which advances through its repeated failure to bring its positing of being (*affirmation*) to fulfillment in any particular, finite positing of a being (*représentation*), always already anticipates the "demand" for an infinite divine Being, which would correspond to its *capacitas entis*.[9]

The modernist and dynamist approaches no doubt

[8] Maurice Blondel's *Carnets Intimes* (Paris: Cerf, 1961), which he wrote during the composition of *L'Action*, nevertheless shows that beneath the philosophical (and we might say "apologetic") outer garments hides a pure and holy Augustinian *cor inquietum*, and that this heart has already surrendered all of its striving toward God in a humble fiat of loving indifference.

[9] Maréchal, too, has in mind something that lies behind and beyond the philosophical dynamism, namely, the mystic's intuition, however veiled, of absolute Being. All philosophy is ultimately a courtyard, indeed an inspired access, to this intuition. Cf. *Mélanges Maréchal*, 1 (1950): 23f. and his early writings that have been republished in that volume.

reflect a great Christian tradition: God, who conde-
scends graciously to his creature, does not want to
lay hold of him and fulfill him in an external manner,
but rather in the most intimate way possible. Historical revelation in the Son aims at a transformative subjective appropriation; its goal is the revelation of the
Holy Spirit of freedom and adoption within the human spirit. The Church Fathers already insisted that
all objective redemption would be useless if it were
not relived subjectively as a dying and rising with
Christ in the Holy Spirit; this truth echoes over and
over throughout the Middle Ages (Bernard, Eckart,
etc.) and the Baroque period.

> Wird Christus tausendmal zu Bethlehem geboren
> Und nicht in dir, du bleibst doch ewiglich verloren . . .
> Das Kreuz zu Golgotha kann dich nicht von dem
>   Bösen,
> Wo es nicht auch in dir wird aufgericht', erlösen.[10]

Paul himself spoke of the Christian's bearing the
stamp of Christ, and spiritual writers have gone
dangerously to the limit, and even beyond, in seeing "holy" Christians as "other Christs" (Francis).
Moreover, even the proof for the existence of God
that is based on the fulfillment of a need (the spirit's

---

[10] "If Christ were born a thousand times in Bethlehem, but not in
you, you would remain lost forever. . . . The Cross on Golgotha cannot redeem you from evil if it is not raised up also in you" (Angelus
Silesius: *Cherubinischer Wandersmann*, 1:61–62; cf. 5:160; 2:81; 5:325).

capacitas entis, which remains unfulfilled in the finite creature) has a long Christian history and even can confidently appeal to Thomas Aquinas for support.[11] Nevertheless, the tradition never set the criterion for the truth of revelation in the center of the pious human subject, it never measured the abyss of grace by the abyss of need or sin, it never judged the content of dogma according to its beneficial effects on human beings. The Spirit does not reveal himself; he reveals the Father in the Son, who has become man. And the Son never allows himself to become reabsorbed in the human spirit—and not even in the Holy Spirit.

Yet another path leads out from the crossroads in Kant, and it is on this path that we find the people who most warrant our serious consideration: those who strove resolutely to make the abstract principles of Idealism concrete. Does the chasm between the empirical man and ideal humanity not yawn so wide for the simple reason that no individual can be humanity by himself? In order to gain an insight into humanity, the individual must encounter an *other*. Ludwig Feuerbach expressed this quite plainly. The human being exists only in relation to others; he truly *is* only in the reciprocity of an I and Thou. The

[11] In laying the foundation for his anthropology, Aquinas bases his proof for the existence of God intellectually on the dynamism of the *desiderium naturale* for the vision of God (*CG* 3:25), and ethically on the dynamism of the desire for *beatitudo perfecta* (*ST* I, II, 99, 2–3).

otherness of the other is a fundamental fact that he must acknowledge if there is to be any possibility of forming a harmonious community in the commonality of human nature, which Feuerbach admittedly identifies all too quickly with the "eternal in us". This otherness of the other in fact leads Feuerbach to the old principle of analogy from the Lateran Council (though he of course rejects it as a figment of the imagination): "The resemblance between the Creator and the creature is such that their still greater dissimilarity cannot fail to be observed."[12] According to Feuerbach, we must recognize that the *actual* individual human being is not merely the key to nature as a whole, but also the sole object of philosophy: philosophy is in the end nothing other than anthropology.[13] It therefore follows that "the new philosophy is founded on the truth of love, . . . Where love is lacking, there can be no truth."[14] Only in the love of the other *as* other, wherein the I passes wholly beyond itself into the sphere of the Thou, can we find the way from man to mankind.

Marx branches off from this point, but so do the personalists and the religious (both Christian and non-Christian) socialists of the twentieth century, Ferdinand Ebner, Martin Buber, and Leonard

[12] *The Essence of Christianity*, Introduction, chapter 2 (*Werke, 1903–1911*, 6:32). Cf. Denz., 432.

[13] *Grundsätze der Philosophie der Zukunft*, no. 54 (1843), *Werke*, 2:317.

[14] Ibid., nos. 34–35, 2:299.

Ragaz.[15] Man sustains himself—indeed, he first comes to himself—in an encounter. When one man meets another face to face, truth comes to pass, the depths of human existence come to light spontaneously, in freedom and in grace. These depths are so unfathomable that Feuerbach, and later, Scheler, identify them with the divine. Anthropology, at this point, transforms from abstract dialectic to concrete

[15] A weaker form of this powerful movement can be found in a certain typical Catholic personalism, which, inspired by Scheler's middle period, reached its peak after World War I in the youth movement and which still has some lingering adherents. This personalism is primarily concerned with the formation of the "Christian personality" in "free self-responsibility", as this comes to expression in free encounters with other people, other cultural values, other religious communities, and finally with the Church. In this version of Christianity, the Cross either appears as part of an "organic ascesis", or it forms the regrettable epilogue of a "partnership", which was begun, under better auspices, between God and man in the Old and New (reciprocally formed) Covenant. In the liturgical movement, we find, paradoxically, another version of this same manner of thinking, insofar as the legitimate desire for more lay participation at the altar surreptitiously turned into an experience of the self and the religious community's enjoyment of its own spirit—a transformation that is reflected even in the new architecture. Finally, there is a popular form, which ultimately stems from Romantic cosmological theology, of an "organological" theology of the *corpus mysticum*, which connects the "member" of the Body of Christ, now sanctified through sacrament and virtue, directly and without any distance, to the Head—whether this is understood in a "spiritual way" (aristocratically) or a cosmic way (democratically), either in relation to the "*Ecclesia*" understood as an eschatological Jerusalem or in relation to the universal Incarnation of God in the whole of the cosmos (Teilhard de Chardin).

dialogical thought. No longer do we have interrelated, reciprocally reversing principles; instead, one person encounters the other in his otherness (expressed paradigmatically in the encounter between the sexes). This hard collision of strangers, this reciprocal resistance—rather than forcing one person on the other through physical or intellectual power—compels the two to be joined in a truth that transcends their finitude.

While everywhere else the anthropological reduction ends in a human being who understands himself and thereby also lays hold of the world and God—all the more so the more fundamentally the cosmos is robbed of its religious significance—here something like a reference beyond opens up: if God, the Wholly-Other, ever wishes to encounter man, the place he manifests himself cannot but lie in the person who remains ever "other" to me, in other words, my "neighbor", who, though nearest to me, is always at the same time the one who stands furthest from me, because no matter how much I can know and experience "about him" or "from him" or "through him", I can never know or experience the person himself in his uniqueness. If God had come only as the "Spirit" who is more interior to me than I am to myself, then he would never have appeared in his essential otherness. He can come as "Spirit" only in order to confirm, to explain, and to communicate his otherness, his "Word", which comes from above, from beyond me, indeed, from the Other.

This is only an intimation, not a deduction from the conditions of possibility of revelation. Its inadequacy becomes apparent the moment we consider that two human beings, however different they may be from one another, nevertheless always encounter one another within the same "nature"; for nature cannot be bracketed out from what it means to be a person. While there is no such thing as "personology", psychology and humanistic studies ("Geisteswissenschaft") certainly exist, and the reciprocal revelation in love becomes coextensive with the understanding we can achieve on the basis of nature. This is why even this personalist form of anthropology cannot be a reference point for an understanding of revelation. Christian revelation cannot be categorially structured even in terms of the dialogical principle.[16] Human beings share a common language, even if each person can leave his own creative stamp on it. But between God and man—when it is a matter of genuine personal self-disclosure and not only a

---

[16] The danger here can be seen in Emil Brunner's *Wahrheit als Begegnung* (1938). Cf. also the work of Dietrich von Hildebrand, Gabriel Marcel, August Brunner, and the work of Martin Buber, which is founded on the principle of dialogue (*Werke*, 1: 1962). For a purely philosophical version, see Karl Jaspers' *Philosophie*, vol. 2 (1932); for more literature, see the article "Ich-Du-Verhältnis", *RGG* III (1959) (Theunissen).

vague, closed knowledge *about* the other—the only language possible is the Word of God, and this language is possible only if God freely chooses to make himself intelligible to man in his Word by interpreting to him the Word that he speaks.[17]

On the margins of the modern anthropological reduction stand two figures whose fundamental aspiration was to show how it is possible, from within the principle of subjectivity, to receive the Word of God that cannot be reduced to subjectivity. Thus, we see Hamann, the sworn enemy of the rationalistic Enlightenment, whose deepest intention—however much his peculiar style obscured it—was to clear space so that the form of the slave would be visible in God's eternally unfathomable self-abasing love. But, above all, we have Søren Kierkegaard, who begins with the principle of dialogue (he speaks in the pseudonyms that converse among themselves; he speaks in his monologues to Regina Olsen, to whom he explains himself; and, finally, he speaks alone with

[17] Here it becomes quite clear why Karl Barth, in founding everything on God's Word and its self-interpretation through man, rejects the *"analogia entis"*. But it would have sufficed for his purposes (as it has in this study so far) simply to reject the *reduction* of revelation to a prior understanding of God's existence on the basis of reason, i.e., to an understanding of "the divine". Someone who has never met a stranger, never spoken to him, never been introduced to him, can still say that he "knows" that stranger, insofar as he knows something about him—and yet it would be just as legitimate to say that he does not know him.

God), "gesticulating with the whole of his subjectivity": in other words, he turns his subjectivity into
a pure sign that he has perceived the absolute sign
of God in the absolute paradox of Christ, a sign
that lies outside and beyond himself. Though he,
too, also says that "truth is subjectivity", he means
that truth occurs in appropriation rather than in an
orthodox or Hegelian speculative objectivity. The
principle of subjectivity has the opposite meaning in
Kierkegaard that it has in Schleiermacher: if Schleiermacher presented Christology as a function of "pious self-consciousness", with Kierkegaard religious
consciousness has become a function of the absolute
paradox, which is grasped in faith and which can in
no way be derived from the self. This is precisely
"the difference between the genius and the apostle".[18] If a man could become in the very depths of
his subjectivity an apostle, a pure instrument of the
one who sent him, then it might be possible through
this subjectivity to make the paradox credible in a
Christian way: the paradox that God is *a* human being, *this* particular man swallowed up by history.

Next to Kierkegaard, a few other witnesses emerge:
Léon Bloy, with the same dual rejection of the
pharisaical objectivism of complacent orthodoxy and
pharisaical sanctity-subjectivism (Huysmans, etc.),
who pointed in the same way to the paradox of

[18] In *The Present Age* (Fontana Library, 1962).

the Cross; Dostoevski in *The Insulted and the Injured*, *The Idiot*, and *The Brothers Karamazov*; and Georges Rouault, who tried over and over again to catch a glimpse, in the fool and the clown, of the head "all covered with blood and wounds".

Here marks the end of the anthropological reduction, even in its most serious, most dialogical, and most existential forms. But even with Kierkegaard's gesticulating with his entire subjectivity, not everything is done. For, if we cannot verify God's Sign in terms of the world or in terms of man, then what else do we have? If we reflect for a moment on the history that has just been sketched out, the question is not as traditional as it would appear to ordinary Christian thinking. There is no text that offers a "foundation" for God's text, making it legible and intelligible, or perhaps we should say more legible and more intelligible. It must interpret itself, and this is what it wishes to do. If it should do so, then there is one thing we can be sure of from the outset: it will not consist in anything that man could have figured out about the world, about himself, and about God, on his own—whether a priori or a posteriori, whether easily or with difficulty, whether as something always already evident, or as a notion that evolves through history.

3. The Third Way of Love

Neither religious philosophy nor existence can provide the criterion for the genuineness of Christianity. In philosophy, man discovers what is humanly knowable about the depths of being; in existence, man lives out what is humanly livable. But Christianity disappears the moment it allows itself to be dissolved into a transcendental precondition of human self-understanding in thinking or living, knowledge or deed. It thus seems at first that the extrinsicist and historical approach of the newer apologetics is the only way forward. This approach does not altogether collapse before philosophy and existence, but only because they both serve to justify the approach in a secondary and subsequent sense. Once the act of faith has been carried out as faith in the historical kerygma, it fulfills metaphysics and ethics even as it elevates them.

Is there thus no path between the Scylla of extrinsicism and the Charybdis of immanentism? Is it not possible to perceive Christianity in such a way that, avoiding both the "blind faith" of the simple (*haplousteroi*) and the gnostic pretensions of those who understand (*gnostikoi*), we could perceive the genuine evidence of the light that breaks forth from revelation without at the same time reducing that light to the measure and laws of human perception?

Two approaches suggest themselves, which nevertheless converge into a unity: on the one hand, there is the personalism we discussed above. No I possesses the possibility or the right to master intellectually the freedom of the Thou that comes out to meet him, to deduce and understand ahead of time the way the Thou will act. I can "understand"[1] a love that has been given to me only as a miracle; I cannot understand it through empirical or transcendental analysis, not even in terms of knowledge about the human "nature" that includes us both— for the Thou will always remain an "other" to me.

The second approach lies in the aesthetic sphere, which represents a third, irreducible realm next to that of thought and action. In the experiences of extraordinary beauty—whether in nature or in art— we are able to grasp a phenomenon in its distinctiveness that otherwise remains veiled. What we encounter in such an experience is as overwhelming as a miracle, something we will never get over. And yet it possesses its intelligibility precisely *as* a mira-

---

[1] The moment I claim to have *understood* the love that another person has for me, i.e., either explaining it on the basis of the laws of human nature or considering myself entitled to it because of my inherent qualities, I have once and for all undermined and falsified that love and thereby cut off the possibility of reciprocation. Genuine love is always inconceivable, and only thus is it a gift.

cle; it is something that binds and frees at the same time, since it gives itself unambiguously as the "self-manifesting freedom" (Schiller) of inner, undemonstrable necessity. *If* Mozart's *Jupiter* symphony has a finale—which is something that I cannot anticipate, derive, or explain on the basis of anything within myself—then it can be only the finale that it has; the symphony possesses its own necessity in this particular form, in which no note could be changed, unless it be by Mozart himself. Such a convergence of what I cannot have invented and yet at the same time what possesses compelling plausibility for me is something we find only in the realm of disinterested beauty. Admittedly, the plausibility of all worldly beauty remains limited by the common worldly nature of the object and subject; "attunement" and competence play an indispensable role, and thus the aesthetic, just like the personal encounter, can serve at best as a sign of Christianity. But this sign is valid to the extent that, just as in mutual human love, where the other *as* other is encountered in a freedom that will never be brought under my control, so too in aesthetic perception it is impossible to reduce the appearing form [*Gestalt*] to my own power of imagination. In both cases, "to understand" what reveals itself does not mean to subsume it under master categories; neither love in the freedom of its grace nor the beautiful in its gratuitousness are things "to be produced" (Rilke), least of all on the basis of a "need" on the part of the subject. Such a reduction to a "need" would be the cynical destruction of love through selfishness; only in the acknowledgment of the pure grace of being loved can the lover also claim to be fulfilled by that love. To dispel the charm of beauty by reducing its "appearance" into some "truth" lying behind or above it is to eliminate beauty altogether and to show that it was never really perceived in its distinctiveness.

The two approaches converge. Already in the realm of nature, eros is the chosen place of beauty: whatever we love—no matter how profoundly or superficially we may love it—always appears radiant with glory; and whatever is objectively perceived as glorious—no matter how profoundly or superficially we experience it—does not penetrate into the onlooker except through the specificity of an eros. Both reciprocally related poles are transcended in the realm of revelation, wherein God's kenotically condescending Logos expresses himself as Love, *Agapē*, and thus as Glory.

John's designation of Christ as the Logos points to the fact that the evangelist envisions him as fulfilling the role of cosmic reason, in the Greeks' and in Philo's sense as that which grants all things their intelligibility. The subsequent events of the Gospel reveal, however, that John does not seek to demonstrate this by projecting the life of Jesus onto the level of Greek wisdom (or vice versa), but rather al-

lows the incarnate Logos to interpret himself. The
Logos reveals himself as "gracious love" (χάρις),
and thereby as "glory" (the "divinely beautiful",
δόξα), and precisely for this reason as the "truth"
(ἀληθείας: Jn 1:14). It therefore becomes possible to
arrive at an intelligibility that illuminates the pure
facticity of the historical as a necessity, and at the
same time an intelligibility that cannot be reduced to
that which the human being demands or (for whatever reason) anticipates.

If the fundamental word of this Logos were not
love—and, indeed, absolute (un-conditional) and
therefore utterly free love, because it is a word that
reveals God—then the Christian Logos would have
to stand as one of a series with the logoi of other
religious wisdom teachings. These teachings fulfill
partial perspectives by (philosophically, gnostically,
or mystically) opening up access to the treasures of
absolute knowledge. The subject's initiation into absolute wisdom, however, no matter how much it
can be experienced as an event of grace, can ultimately be understood only in a Socratic-maieutic
manner (as Kierkegaard shows in relation to Hegel).
But if the fundamental word is not only "love"
but "*divine* love", then the fundamental aesthetic
word "glory" must accompany it, since this word
preserves the distance of the Wholly-Other within
God's self-manifestation as love, and absolutely pre-
vents us from confusing this love with any other

(even personal) love that claims to be absolute. The plausibility of God's love does not become apparent through any comparative reduction to what man has always already understood as love; rather, it is illuminated only by the self-interpreting revelation-form of love itself. And this form is so majestic that we are led to adore it from a reverent distance whenever we perceive it, even if it does not explicitly command us to do so.

The majesty of absolute love, which is the most fundamental phenomenon of revelation, is the source of any authority human mediators may possess. The original authority is possessed neither by the Bible (as the written "Word of God") nor by the kerygma (as the living proclamation of the "Word of God") nor by ecclesial office (as official representation of the "Word of God"): all three are "merely" word, and thus not yet flesh. The Old Testament too, as "Word", is merely advancing toward ultimate authority. The sole authority is the Son, who interprets the Father in the Holy Spirit as divine Love. For it is only here, at the source of revelation, that authority (or majesty) and love can—and necessarily do—coincide. All that the demand for obedient faith to revelation can do is thus prepare man to perceive the manifestation of God's love and to give it its due.[2] Divine Love can appear in such an over-

---

[2] Characteristically, Greek has no word that corresponds to the

whelming way that its glorious majesty throws one to the ground; it shines out as the last word and leaves one no choice but to respond in the mode of pure, blind obedience. Nevertheless, both the word and the response acquire their meaning only through a gift from the eternal Person to the finite person, a gift that includes the ability to respond as a finite creature to the infinite, and whose heart and essence is love.

The majesty of absolute Love that approaches man in revelation goes out to meet him, invites him, and elevates him to an inconceivable intimacy. It allows the finite spirit to understand for the first time what it really means to say that God is the Wholly-Other, that he is "in reality and in essence, distinct from the world, supremely happy in himself and from himself, and inexpressibly loftier than anything besides himself which either exists or can

---

Latin "*auctoritas*" (which incidentally indicates in the first place "authentication", a beneficial guarantee, a helping influence, weighty recommendation, advice, exhortation, and so forth, and only secondarily authentically expresses opinion, command, and authority). For αἰδώς is deferential shame, ἀξίωσις is primarily subjective esteem or recognition (and only for this reason objective superiority), and τιμή likewise means subjective estimation, assessment, valuation, and therefore respect and finally objective value.

Ecclesial authority, as the "razing of all defenses against God", is according to Paul "taking every thought captive in the obedience of Christ" (2 Cor 10:5), in the twofold sense of being obedient to the obedient Christ.

be imagined" (Vat. I, ss. 3, c. 1). Apart from this revelation of love, all negative theology remains so empty that it is in immediate danger of drifting either into atheism (or agnosticism) or a philosophy (or mysticism) of identity. By contrast, once we see that the figure of revelation remains unintelligible unless it is interpreted in light of God's love, then the Wholly-Other and Ever-Greater *appears* tangibly and surprises us in the ultimate and unsurpassable incomprehensibility of divine love. Precisely in the movement in which the creature sees and feels itself drawn to God's heart, it knows in its most unfathomable depths that it is not God, and it grasps in an undeniable and irrevocable way the fundamental difference, which is never to be closed, between absolute and relative, divine and worldly being. And yet the creature can endure the tremors that this difference sends through the foundations of its finitude only when it has understood how to read the figure of revelation: not merely in terms of form as "Word", but also in terms of content as absolute Love. Only the New Testament shows this:[3] on

---

[3] It thus stands in contrast to the Old Testament, in which God's Word remains essentially a promise even when it comes to pass. The Old Testament therefore remains formally within an (abstracting) vacillation between election and rejection and for this reason holds the responding faith in an (abstract) suspension that is distinct from love. Nevertheless, we ought not overlook the extent to which this form points dynamically to the New Testament. In this respect, it is already evident (and will become even clearer later) that there cannot be a formal principle of Scripture in the New Testament sense, nor can

the one hand, love is not merely one divine property *juxtaposed* to others—which would make man's
love in response merely one virtue *juxtaposed* to others. (The theological insight into *caritas* as *forma virtutum* immediately implies *caritas* as *forma revelationis*.)
On the other hand, love cannot therefore be seen as
connected to fear in a "unity of opposites", for in
the New Testament, "fear" takes its form and measure from the reverence (*timor filialis*) that is owed
to the love that manifests itself precisely in *such* a
way.

We can see that what we have been discussing is
truly a third way once we compare it with what is
offered as an "orthodox" alternative to modernism:
namely, an "integralism" of an abstract ecclesial disposition, which however does not attempt to inte-
grate the multiplicity of dogmas in a specifically intellectual or spiritual manner, but instead strives to
shut down the opponent through an unintellectual
and unspiritual use of force.[4] The substitution of

Scripture possess the formal authority that the Reformers attribute to
it. This would imply an abstraction—from the Old and New Testament to "Scripture in general"—that is inappropriate in the Biblical
realm and moreover fixes the words of Scripture for all practical purposes in their Old Testament twilight between law and grace. The
principle of *sola scriptura* and double predestination thus turn out to
be two sides of the same coin.

[4] Cf. in this regard, Maurice Blondel's outstanding essay (written anonymously): "La Semaine Sociale de Bordeaux et le Mono-
phorisme" (Paris: Blond, 1910), and Daniel-Rops' "Une crise de

violent means for intelligence or spirit suggests that a genuine solution on an intellectual and spiritual level lay at that time out of reach.

The third way is indivisible, since we interpret and understand the form of Christian revelation either wholly in terms of the self-glorification of absolute love or else we simply fail to understand it. In this respect, Rousselot's theory of the "eyes of faith"[5] was correct: either one sees it or one does not; but the power to see the glory of love requires at least a seed of supernatural love.[6] Nevertheless, this does not rule out (1) the possibility of being scandalized (as a refusal to acknowledge the radiant evidence and to respond by following the path of self-surrender) or (2) the possibility of a groping rational approach toward the decisive vision: the lines of the kerygma and the gospel visibly converge at a point that nevertheless remains "invisible", that is, a transcendental point of unity that cannot yet be fully presumed or taken for granted.

---

l'esprit: le Modernisme (in *La Table Ronde*, Nov./Dec. 1962). The documents of the integralist and anti-modernist center La Sapinière are currently [as of 1963] being prepared for publication.

[5] [English translation: *The Eyes of Faith* (New York: Fordham University Press, 1990).]

[6] No one has described this better than Pascal, in the parts of the *Pensées* treating biblical revelation. See my essay "Les yeux de Pascal", in *Pascal et Port Royal* (Paris: Fayard, 1962).

4. The Failures of Love

When man encounters the love of God in Christ, not only does he experience what genuine love is, but he is also confronted with the undeniable fact that he, a selfish sinner, does not himself possess true love. He experiences two things at once: the finitude of the creature's love and its sinful frigidity. To be sure, he does possess something of an "anticipation" [*Vorverständnis*] of what love is; if he did not, he would not be able to make any sense of the sign of Jesus Christ. Indeed, the sign itself would also be opaque and contradictory in an objective sense, because, here, the love of God has appeared in the form of flesh, that is, in the form of human love. All the same, man cannot come to a recognition of this sign on the basis of his "anticipation" without a radical conversion—a conversion not only of the heart, which must in the face of this love confess that it has failed to love until now, but also a conversion of thought, which must relearn what love after all really is.

First, let us consider the implications of finitude. It is impossible to deny the reality of love that one finds in nature, from its roots in the subhuman realm all the way up to the human. The evidence cannot be gainsaid by any skeptical theory of the will to power or self-fulfillment. We see eros at play beyond the sphere of utility; we see the animal's service and devotion to its young, and the individual's self-renouncing sacrifice for the whole. At the human level, what was an ephemeral relationship enters into the sphere of spiritual and supratemporal significance: the passing moment of eros can be the gateway to a lifelong fidelity that outlasts this particular moment, which allows the relationship to one's young to deepen into a familial love that embraces both nature and spirit; the loss of the individual that passes away in relation to the greater power of the species that endures can give rise to the notion of the individual's self-offering for the sake of the community, the clan, the people or the nation; and in death one can gather up one's entire existence in a gesture of self-renunciation and receive an intimation of the meaning of being itself as love.

But though all of this may point the way, it does not accomplish the journey, for there are other equally strong, or stronger, powers that set a limit to love's movement: the fight for one's place under the sun; the terrible stifling of the individual by the surrounding relations, the clan, and even by the family; the struggle of natural selection, for which nature itself provides the strength and the arms; the laws of time's decay: friendships, once thought to be forever, grow cold, people grow apart, views and perspectives and thus hearts too become estranged. Geographic distances create an additional burden, and love must be strong and single-minded in order to withstand it; pledges of love, meant to be eternal, get broken, because the rising wave of eros gave way and another newer love came in between; the beloved's faults and limitations became unbearable, and perhaps even worsened because the finitude of love seemed to be a contradiction: Why love just one woman when there are thousands that could be loved? Don Juan poses this question as he shakes the cage of finitude, driven by a fundamental intuition no less valid, perhaps, than Faust's. But if the very meaning of love slips past the don in the surfeit of women, Faust fails to hold onto the eternity he thought he could pin down in the surfeit of "moments".

Even in the family, love is circumscribed by the limitations of nature: if this love is initially based on the unconscious bond of blood, the moment the spirit awakens, this same blood-based intimacy can be felt as an obstacle to one's freely carving out one's own place; too much reciprocal insight can spoil the fresh expectation of the gifts to be given; parents may perhaps fail to give room to the freedom that one needs in growing up, insofar as their horizon begins to tighten around their own centers, which lie in a temporal sense elsewhere. And then love for man can be a part of what motivates certain human activities—farming and hunting, management of the state and war, household economy and business, learning and research—but it cannot form these activities from top to bottom and domesticate them. The other forces of existence retain power and domination over against love. When man absolutizes creaturely love at the expense of the agonistic forces of life, he contradicts himself in a biological and cultural sense, as Nietzsche has shown. The sphere of ordinary existence, the place where people interact, contains at best a middle position in which love and self-interest, love and nonlove, temper one another.[1]

The individual's death, which represents a solemn moment for the community since it too experiences the forces of fate that overshadow men, may be something the individual accepts with "resignation", allowing himself to be sent toward his destiny [*eine Schickung in das Geschick*], and it may thus offer some

[1] In their reaction to an abstract humanism of love and virtue, the English Christian freethinkers had a sober insight into this: Hobbes in a more radical way, Locke and ethical liberalism in a more moderate way, and Bernard Mandeville, without compromise. The endeavor to moralize the human being through and through is questionable, given man's roots in the animal realm. Even viewed as a historical and cultural process, such an endeavor seems to belie a hidden (spiritualistic) attack on the balance of nature as a whole. Something like the Augustinian-Pascalian analysis of existence as *concupiscentia* has to be reckoned with already at the natural level.

glimmer of the wisdom and kindness behind it. But
—no matter what the thinkers influenced by Christianity have claimed—the convergence of such a resignation with personal, human love nevertheless lies
beyond the horizon of human nature. Death may
usher a person into a realm of immortality, and therefore judgment, which, frightening as it may be, is
nevertheless purifying, a realm that is somehow divine and eternal; and the soul may expect to meet a
good destiny therein. Nevertheless, the entire process, comprising each individual moment, cannot be
addressed by the name of love. And this becomes all
the more impossible the more a personal Providence
is called into question with the fading of personal
images of the gods and later the fading of the divine
glory of the mythological cosmos. Even in the Old
Testament, which places the love between the Lord
of the Covenant and the people of the Covenant (and
therein creation as a whole) into the center of the
meaning of existence, death and the realm beyond
remain a vague afterthought on the margins.

Finally, human love shares in the insoluble contradiction of an existence that is at once mortal and
spiritual: personal love, which lovers swear to one
another in exalted moments, means a definitiveness
that outlasts death; but "eternal love" "for a time"
is an unliveable contradiction. And yet, nothing in
the economy of visible nature ensures a continuation
of human existence (understood as a whole and not

only in relation to the soul), while it is precisely this whole existence, and not a free-floating and inconceivable soul, which was intended by love. Intended, and at the same time not intended, the here and now ought to be eternal—and at the same time ought not to be (lest it become an unbearable hell). Thus, the heart remains a mystery to itself. The exalted moment of love is always full of promise: it is not closed in on itself, but open; we see its natural fruitfulness revealed in the child, even if its spiritual fruitfulness remains hidden. Human love, in its purely creaturely dimension, is a hieroglyph; in grammatical terms, it is always an inchoative, which never allows itself properly to be translated into the indicative mood.

Second, the implications of sin. We have already observed that sin stands out in its proper contours only in the light of Christian revelation. It is only when we look the Crucified One in the eye that we recognize the abyss of selfishness—even of that which we are accustomed to call love. When the question is most seriously put to us, we say No where Christ, out of love, said Yes, and in our nonlove, we say Yes without a second thought to Jesus' bearing of our sins: How can we have a problem with it, if it is something he wants to do? But this is precisely why God does not ask the sinner to agree to the Cross; he seeks consent to the most terrible death of the beloved only from those that love (Jn 12:7; cf. Lk 1:38; Jn 20:17). The event of the

Passion exposes the truth of humanity—made up of Christians, Jews, and pagans. As the mask is mercilessly torn away, "every mouth falls silent", and "every man" who speaks of love proves himself "a liar": "None is righteous, no, not one; . . . all have turned aside, no one seeks for God, . . . the way of peace they do not know, there is no fear of God before their eyes" (Rom 3:4-19, passim).

But already among men in general there is an awareness of failure, that cannot be brought out into the open and settled through the balancing out of fault and repentance. If this were sufficient, one would always be able to restore perfect goodness and justice. But at a deeper level, man is aware of his heart's paralysis, fallenness, and frigidity, his incapacity to meet the demand of any law of love, no matter how generally postulated. He simply cannot summon up enough courage for it. And in any event he would not presume to believe in such a fulfillment of existence. He finds such a lack of strength in himself that he thinks he must complain to authorities higher than his own heart, a heart that to be sure could always go a few steps further than it actually does, but could never (it feels quite certain about this) make the entire journey—all the more so insofar as no one can really imagine where this path may in fact lead. The stages of the journey are impossible to map out; they trail off immediately into the impenetrable night. Thus, he lets go of guilt in a

is either dispensable or it plays a merely intermediate role, clearing and lighting up the way to total knowledge.

We can thus already see that Christianity, as a genuine revealed religion, cannot be a communication of knowledge, a "teaching", in the first place, but only secondarily. It must be in the first place an action that God undertakes, the playing out of the drama that God began with mankind in the Old Covenant. The content of this action cannot in any essential way be derived from or anticipated a priori on the basis of created nature, because it arises from the Other *as* Other in unfathomable freedom toward his other; no preliminary bridge of understanding can be built on similarity or, for that matter, on identity. The key to understanding the action lies solely in God's presentation of himself to human beings on the stage of human nature, by virtue of the identity of the divine "Author", the divine and human "Actor", and the divine Spirit, who exists identically in both and who interprets the action for those whom the Actor has brought into the drama. Just because God's Covenant is his battle of love *with* sinful man does not mean that this battle of love can be understood and assessed *by* man. Indeed, the fact that God's love transforms him, converting him or hardening his heart, expresses not the essence of that love, but its effect. It would be a peculiar lover who sought to measure the love of his bride by how much her love benefited or injured him. God's action on man's behalf is, instead, "intelligible" only insofar as it is *not* understood and justified in terms of incomplete anthropological and cosmological fragments; in the light of such standards, it cannot but appear as "foolishness" and "madness".

There can be no possibility of working out a speculative interpretation of this "foolishness", because that would mean reducing the sphere of the translogical "whylessness" of the personal gift of love (that is, the sphere of the Holy Spirit) back to the sphere of the Logos, understood as comprehensive cosmological and anthropological reason. But this misinterprets the "Trinity of salvation history" as the Manifestation of the Absolute.[2]

Man is caught in a strange predicament: he can, if

---

[2] The Jesuit Georges Morel's attempt to interpret John of the Cross in Hegelian terms is therefore already completely misguided, for the absolute uniqueness of the One God's loving revelation to the unique persons of the saints cannot be reduced to general ontological and rational categories ("Le sens de l'existence selon S. Jean de la Croix", 1–3, [Paris: Aubier, 1960–1961]). It is at the very least dangerous for Gaston Fessard, S.J., to interpret Ignatius' *Exercises* according to Hegel (*La Dialectique des Exercices spirituels de S. Ignace de Loyola* [Paris: Aubier, 1956]). If it is no doubt true that God's self-disclosure in the Covenant occurs within the dialectical structure of the world-historical logos, nevertheless God is never himself this logos. The reflective Christian can assure himself of this fact, whether he does so in dialectical or *existentiell* categories. Erich Przywara is therefore quite correct, in his *Analogia Entis* (1–2, 1962), to allow the entire dialectic of worldly thinking in philosophy and theology to consume itself in flame—in relation to the constantly growing and never-to-be-mastered mystery of divine love.

he is honest, "conceptualize" God only as Wholly-Other rather than as worldly being. And yet, if in spite of this God should become manifest, he still desires to see him only as a kind of superabundant fulfillment of all cosmology and anthropology. For he cannot leap over his spiritual horizon on his own; only the Wholly-Other can make this possible. And if this transcendence actually takes place, then God's action can break in upon him only as a "wholly other" truth and wisdom—not merely in the "first shock", since this is an experience one eventually gets over, but essentially and always anew. And he can receive therein the inconceivable fulfillment of his being, at most, only along with the abiding shock. But to feel the shock in this way cannot occur merely at the upper limits of his experience of being—where man for the most part expects it because it is there that the human seems to flow into the divine—but rather right there, immediately in front of his nose, in the *concretissimum* of human existence. A stone stands before him, obstructing his path, and there is no way he can avoid crashing into it in the hardest and most frustrating way, so that, in stumbling, he is forced to see he is without a foothold.

But, unless he blindly takes offense at the offense, he can interpret this "trap" (*scandalum*) that God has set for him only as God's love, a love that runs after him, pulls him out of the pit, casts aside his chains and places him in the freedom of divine and now even human love. Because of his dim "pre-understanding" of love, he can prick up his ears at the sound of the message of absolute love and perceive the image to which this message points. Stumbling into the trap, however, first makes it clear to him that neither the existence nor the essence of the love offering itself to him belongs to him by nature. The scandal is here to draw his eye to the uniqueness of the love that manifests itself and, in its light, to reveal his own inchoate, creaturely love quite concretely for the nonlove that it is.[3]

---

[3] Pre-Christian "cosmological" gnosis can be forgiven insofar as God's word of love had not yet sounded for it. By contrast, when gnosis is deliberately posited over against the love of Christ as the higher and more comprehensive perspective, it becomes a straightforward and conscious rejection of love, and it thus incurs guilt (Jn 15:22).

5. Love Must Be Perceived

If God wishes to reveal the love that he harbors for the world, this love has to be something that the world can recognize, in spite of, or in fact *in*, its being wholly other. The inner reality of love can be recognized only by love. In order for a selfish beloved to understand the selfless love of a lover (not only as something he can use, which happens to serve better than other things, but rather as what it truly is), he must already have some glimmer of love, some initial sense of what it is. Similarly, a person who contemplates a great work of art has to have a gift—whether inborn or acquired through training—to be able to perceive and assess its beauty, to distinguish it from mediocre art or kitsch. This preparation of the subject, which raises him up to the revealed object and tunes him to it, is for the individual person the disposition we could call the threefold unity of faith, hope, and love, a disposition that must already be present at least in an inchoative way in the very first genuine encounter. And it can be thus present because the love of God, which is of course grace, necessarily includes in itself its own conditions of recognizability and therefore brings this possibility with it and communicates it.

After a mother has smiled at her child for many days and weeks, she finally receives her child's smile in response. She has awakened love in the heart of her child, and as the child awakens to love, it also awakens to knowledge: the initially empty-sense impressions gather meaningfully around the core of the Thou. Knowledge (with its whole complex of intuition and concept) comes into play, because the play of love has already begun beforehand, initiated by the mother, the transcendent. God interprets himself to man as love in the same way: he radiates love, which kindles the light of love in the heart of man, and it is precisely this light that allows man to perceive this, the absolute Love: "For it is the God who said, 'Let light shine out of darkness', who has shown in our hearts to give the light of the knowledge of the glory of God in the face of Christ" (2 Cor 4:6). In this face, the primal foundation of being smiles at us as a mother and as a father. Insofar as we are his creatures, the seed of love lies dormant within us as the image of God (*imago*). But just as no child can be awakened to love without being loved, so too no human heart can come to an understanding of God without the free gift of his grace—in the image of his Son.

Prior to an individual's encounter with the love of God at a particular time in history, however, there has to be another, more fundamental and archetypal encounter, which belongs to the conditions of possibility of the appearance of divine love to man. There has to be an encounter, in which the *unilateral* movement of God's love toward man is understood as such and that means also appropriately received and answered. If man's response were not suited to the love offered, then it would not in fact be revealed (for, this love cannot be revealed merely ontologically, but must be revealed at the same time in a spiritual and conscious way). But if God could not take this response for granted from the outset, by including it within the unilateral movement of his grace toward man, then the relationship would be bilateral from the first, which would imply a reduction back into the anthropological schema. The Holy Scriptures, taken in isolation, cannot provide the word of response, because the letter kills when it is separated from the spirit, and the letter's inner spirit is God's word and not man's answer. Rather, it can be only the living response of love from a human spirit, as it is accomplished in man through God's loving grace: the response of the "Bride", who in grace calls out, "Come!" (Rev 22:17) and, "Let it be to me according to your word" (Lk 1:38), who "carries within the seed of God" and therefore "does not sin" (1 Jn 3:9), but "kept all of these things, pondering them in her heart" (Lk 2:19, 51). She, the pure one, is "placed, blameless and glorious" (Eph 5:26–27; 2 Cor 11:2) before him, by the blood of God's love, as the "handmaid" (Lk 1:38), as the "lowly servant" (Lk 1:48), and thus as the paradigm of the loving faith that accepts all things (Lk 1:45; 11:28) and "looks to him in reverent modesty, submissive before him" (Eph 5:24, 33; Col 3:18).

Had the love that God poured out into the darkness of nonlove not itself generated this womb (Mary was pre-redeemed by the grace of the Cross; in other words, she is the first fruit of God's self-outpouring into the night of vanity), then this love would never have penetrated the night and it would never in fact have had the capacity to do so (as a serious reading of Luther's *justus-et-peccator* theology illuminates in this regard). To the contrary, an original and creaturely act of letting this be done (*fiat*) has to correspond to this divine event, a bridal *fiat* to the Bridegroom. But the bride must receive herself purely from the Bridegroom (κεχαριτωμένη: Lk 1:28); she must be "brought forward" and "prepared" by him and for him (παριστάναι: 2 Cor 11:2; Eph 5:27)[1] and therefore at his exclusive disposal, offered up to him (as it is expressed in the word παριστάναι; cf. the "presentation" in the temple, Lk 2:22 and Rom 6:13f.; 12:1; Col 1:22, 28).

This originally justified relationship of love (because it does justice to the reality) in itself threads together in a single knot all the conditions for man's perception of divine love: (1) the Church as the spot-

[1] ThWNT, 5:835–40.

less Bride in her core, (2) Mary, the Mother-Bride, as the locus, at the heart of the Church, where the fiat of the response and reception is real, (3) the Bible, which as spirit (-witness) can be nothing other than the Word of God bound together in an indissoluble unity with the response of faith. A "critical" study of this Word as a human, historical document will therefore necessarily run up against the reciprocal, nuptial relationship of word and faith in the witness of the Scripture. The "hermeneutical circle" justifies the formal correctness of the word even before the truth of the content is proven. But it can, and *must*, be shown that, in the relationship of *this* faith to *this* Word, the content of the Word consists in faith, understood as the handmaid's *fiat* to the mystery of the outpouring of divine love. But insofar as the Word of Scripture belongs to the Bride-Church, since she gives articulation to the Word that comes alive in her, then (4) the Bride and Mother, who is the archetype of faith, must proclaim this Word, in a living way, to the individual as the living Word of God; and the function of preaching (as a "holy and serving office"), like the Church herself and even the Word of Scripture, must be implanted by the revelation of God himself, as an answer to that revelation, as it is illuminated by the relationship between the Church and the Bible.

To be sure, the response of faith to revelation, which God grants to the creature he chooses and moves with his love, occurs in such a way that it is truly the creature that provides the response, with its own nature and its natural powers of love. But this occurs only in grace, that is, by virtue of God's original gift of a loving response that is adequate to God's loving Word. And therefore, the creature responds in connection with, and "under the protective mantle" of, the *fiat* that the Bride-Mother, Mary-Ecclesia, utters in an archetypal fashion, once and for all.[2]

---

[2] Augustine offers a magnificent description of the archetypal *prius* of the perfect Yes in the *Confessions* (XII, 15; PL 32, 833): "Do you deny that there is a sublime created realm cleaving with such pure love to the true and truly eternal God that, though not coeternal with him, it never detaches itself from him and slips away into the changes and successiveness of time, but rests in utterly authentic contemplation of him alone? . . . We do not find that time existed before this created realm, for 'wisdom was created before everything' (Eccles. [Sir] 1:4). Obviously this does not mean your wisdom, our God, father of the created wisdom . . . [but] that which is created, an intellectual nature which is light from contemplation of the light. But just as there is a difference between light which illuminates and that which is illuminated, so also there is an equivalent difference between the wisdom which creates and that which is created, as also between the justice which justifies and the justice created by justification. . . . So there was a wisdom created before all things which is a created thing, the rational and intellectual mind of your pure city, our 'mother which is above and is free' (Gal 4:26). . . . O House full of light and beauty! . . . During my wandering may my longing be for you! I ask him who made you that he will also make me his property in you, since he also made me" (*Confessions*, trans. Henry Chadwick [Oxford: Oxford University Press, 1991; reissued as an Oxford World's Classics paperback 1998], 255–56).

It is not necessary to measure the full scope of the faith achieved in human simplicity and in veiled consciousness in the chamber at Nazareth and in the collegium of the apostles. For the unseen seed that was planted here needed the dimensions of the spirit or intellect to germinate: dimensions that, once again, stand out in a fundamental and archetypal way in the Word of Scripture, but which first unfold in the contemplation of the biblical tradition over the course of centuries—"written on the tables of our hearts" and henceforth "to be known and read by all men" (2 Cor 3:2–3), written "in persuasive demonstrations of spirit and power", spirit as power and power as spirit (1 Cor 2:4). That which the "Spirit" of God, however, interprets in our hearts with "power" (and which the Church interprets in "service to the Spirit" [2 Cor 3:8]) is nothing other than God's own outpouring of love in Christ; indeed, the Spirit *is* the outpouring of the Son of God, "the Spirit of the Lord" (2 Cor 3:18), since the Lord himself "is Spirit" (2 Cor 3:17).

When Christ is immediately thereafter designated the "Image of God" (2 Cor 4:4), then this expression ought not to be reduced to mythical terms, since myth was definitively left behind with the dimension of the Incarnation of the Word, which surpassed it. He is the "Image", which is not a merely natural or symbolic expression, but a Word, a free self-communication, and precisely therefore a Word that is always already (in the grace of the Word) heard, understood, and taken in, otherwise, there would be no revelation. There is no such thing as a "dialogical image", except that which exists at the higher level of the Word, although it remains true —and contrary to what Protestant and existential theology may claim—that the Word preserves and elevates in itself all the value of the image at the higher level of freedom. If the Word made man is originally a dialogical Word (and not merely in a second moment), then it becomes clear that even the level of the unilateral (ethical-religious) teaching of knowledge has been surpassed. It is not possible that Christ could have written books ("about" something, whether about himself, about God, or about his teaching); the book "about" him must concern the *trans-action* between him and the man whom he has encountered, addressed, and redeemed in love. This means that the level on which his Holy Spirit expresses himself (in the letter), must necessarily itself be "in the spirit" (of the love of revelation and the love of faith), in order to be "objective" at all. To put it another way, the site from which love can be observed and generated cannot itself lie outside of love (in the "pure logicity" of so-called science); it can lie only there, where the matter itself lies— namely, in the drama of love. No exegesis can dispense with this fundamental principle to the extent that it wishes to do justice to its subject matter.

6. Love as Revelation

If revelation were not love, then a receptive disposition of pure letting-be—which is intelligible only as the attitude of love that allows itself (as faith) to be led beyond all desire for self-knowledge—would be inhuman and unworthy of God, and God's revelation itself would not be able to instill such an attitude as an answer to his Word. Love can accord a priori (and therefore as faith) only with love, never with nonlove. But the conclusion we draw about the Word from the answer already objectively presupposes a conclusion about the answer drawn from the Word: it is only because the Word has already been expressed and understood as love that the response of love can occur, and in this respect the response can be nothing more than opening up a "free pathway" for the Word; it is creation's "nihil obstat" to God, who desires to penetrate into the place where there is nothing but obstat, nothing but pure resistance to his Love. We must now explicate the content of the formal proposition, "Love alone is credible", in both its positive (a) and its negative (b) significance.

a. The life of Jesus presents itself initially as a life of teaching (the meaning of which is explicated through imaginative parables and spiritual deeds), and then as a life of suffering and death. At the same time, however, the radiant absoluteness of the teaching, which shines forth in what it says, promises, and demands, becomes intelligible only in terms of the fact that his life points as a whole toward the Cross. All the acts of self-disclosure in word and deed receive their validity through a Passion that explains everything and makes it all possible. If one sought to understand this Passion as an accident that happened to occur at a certain point through an incidental cause, then every single word, even those of the Sermon on the Mount, would lose its meaning. We cannot take seriously any attempt to separate Jesus' teaching before the Passion, which thus has no relationship to it, from the teaching that is supposedly placed into his mouth after the Passion. The Logos of both his teaching and his action as a whole has to be interpreted in its relationship to "the hour" that he awaits, to the "baptism" he desires, to the event that opens up his prophetic mission, which is to bring the old Jewish Covenant to completion in the new sacrificial Covenant, the new blood of the Covenant, the new Covenantal meal.

Whether directly or indirectly, this teaching points to a self-surrender for "one's friends" (Jn 15:13), for "the many" (Mt 20:28; Mk 10:45), for "all" (Jn

12:32; 17:21); indeed, it points to the decisive form
this self-surrender takes in Jesus. This self-surrender
is by no means the achievement of a single individual, but rather presents itself as a deed that has been
carried out in obedience, as the final act of a life
that spent itself in ever greater self-effacing service
to all men (Lk 22:27; Jn 13:3–17). Just as the teaching receives its logos, its logic, from this sacrificial
death, so too it places the entire existence of all of
his followers under the same "logos of the Cross"
(1 Cor 1:18). This would necessarily imply the can-
celing out of every logos and every logic (because
it places life under the law of death) unless we as-
sumed that Jesus' death, which governs his life, is
as such the act that manifests the "power of God
and the wisdom of God" (1 Cor 1:24), precisely
in its ultimate impotence. This power and wisdom,
however, do not grasp at themselves (see Phil 2:6)
and remain withdrawn, but pour themselves out to
the very end in "powerlessness" and "foolishness"
—and precisely by doing so, as functions of absolute love, they are "more powerful than men" and
"wiser than men" (1 Cor 1:25).

Jesus proclaims himself with his teaching, he is essentially "handed over" (*traditus*) in it; without conditions and without reservations, he aims at a point
beyond all ethics and sociology, a point that lies "no-
where" (*u-topos*) in the world, into which he casts
the whole of his existence, body and soul. And by

casting himself, in gratuitous freedom (Jn 10:18), into this unimaginable abyss (death as abandonment by God [Mt 27:46] or as followed by the underworld [Rev 6:8; 1:18] bereft of all hope), he makes himself into an indispensable sacrificial food for all (Jn 6:51: "My flesh for the life of the world"; Heb 13:10–12), not in the freedom of creative genius but in straightforward obedience (Jn 10:18).

The indissoluble connection between word and act of suffering thus points back at every moment to one who commissions, one whose existence would remain questionable only if we suspected the one commissioned of fanatical religious enthusiasm (or, to put it bluntly, of "insanity"). But the sober tone that penetrates to the very core of his words belies this suspicion, his demeanor is matter-of-fact, there is no fanatical Dionysian exaltation. He never speaks of his self-surrender in tones of ecstatic eros, but rather uses almost deadpan words that point to his obedience: without ever denying his own responsibility, he refers all the initiative and the ultimate responsibility (and therefore the glory of this consummate plan) back to the Father. Obediently identifying himself with his mission, he himself is his mission in person, and therefore, in his kenosis as the "servant of God", he becomes the manifestation of God's eternal love for the world. But, for the same reason, he becomes the manifestation of his eternal majesty and kingship, which reveals itself most definitively in the servant's ultimate humiliation ("Yes, I am a king", Jn 18:37). But if the kingship of the God who reveals himself as love comes to light precisely in the Son's humble obedience to the Father, then it is clear that this obedience is essentially love. It is certainly the paradigmatic attitude of love the creature must have before God's majesty, but far more than that, it is the radiant paradigm of divine love itself: precisely in—and *only* in—the kenosis of Christ, the *inner* mystery of God's love comes to light, the mystery of the God who "is love" (1 Jn 4:8) in himself and therefore is "triune".[1]

Though it remains a light inaccessible to the understanding, God's triunity is the sole hypothesis capable of clarifying the phenomenon of Christ (as he is continuously present in the Bible, in the Church, and in history) in a phenomenologically adequate

---

[1] "For he decided, with the Father and the Holy Spirit, to show the world the glory of his omnipotence *in no other way than through his death*", Anselm, *Cur Deus Homo*, 1:9 (Schmitt, II 62, 23–25). It thus becomes clear in what sense the revelation of God's love in Christ is *"indirect"*. Not only is it true that God appears *only* in man (as the Wholly-Other), but he moreover appears in that dimension of man that is most dissimilar to God. But the sign of contradiction that covers this mystery like a veil is in fact a contradiction only for man in his natural and sinful reason, not for God; and if God in his sovereign freedom chooses this sign as his mode of expression, there can be none more adequate—for him, it is no "paradox". This becomes evident at once if man looks at it in faith from God's perspective. He then can see with certainty (*certitudo fidei*) that God's love, in its inconceivability, has found the most eloquent of all words.

manner, without doing violence to the facts.[2] If it were not the case that the Absolute is love (which is something only the doctrine of the Trinity affirms), then the Absolute would remain merely Logos (νόησις νοήσεως, absolute knowledge), which either comes to a stop *before* love and therefore remains extrinsic to it or would always already have surpassed it, in a modern, titanic fashion, and "digested" it into itself. But this would be possible only by reducing love to the sphere of "understanding" [*Verstand*], thereby killing the (Holy) Spirit [*Geist*].

The synoptic Gospels bear clear witness to the fact that, from the beginning, as Jesus revealed God's love, he trained men in the Spirit of divine love—leading them beyond their own criteria and certainties in "faith". In the course of his introducing them into the Spirit, Jesus withdraws his bodily, earthly presence ("It is to your advantage that I go away", Jn 16:7), so that his and the Father's Spirit may come, who, as the fullness of love, simultaneously fulfills and testifies to this kenotic self-effacement in

---

[2] Wherever a genuine revelation of God (as he is in himself) through the revelation of Christ and his Church is intended in Scripture—that is, practically everywhere—then what is thereby intended is necessarily an absolute image of God in the economic order. To act as if Paul, for example, had "merely" an economic Trinity in mind betrays as much theological poverty as that dogmatic theology which negligently entangles the immanent Trinity in a net of categories without remaining, both formally and materially, within the *event* in which the Trinity manifests itself in the economic order.

love. That is why every "separation through death" (which occurs on Holy Saturday) is altogether overcome in the "Ascension". Jesus was not "missed" by the generation that came after, because "God's love has been poured into our hearts through the Holy Spirit which has been given to us" (Rom 5:5); it is for this reason that Paul no longer wishes to know Jesus "in the flesh" (2 Cor 5:16). This does not mean that we have left behind the place where the Spirit was given to us, but it does mean that the chosen place wherein eternal love was manifest in time will be taken up into a spiritual and omnitemporal relation. In the ever-present Anamnesis ("Do this in memory of me", 1 Cor 11:25) of the self-sacrifice of God's love (*unde et memores*), the living and resurrected Christ becomes present (Mt 18:20)—but present "until he comes again" (1 Cor 11:26), and therefore not looking backward, but with eyes set forward, into the future and full of hope. Only nonfaith and nonlove can imprison Christians in their past; the Spirit has set them free to enter into every age and every future; indeed, they move forward, fashioning and transforming the world in everything they do in the light of the abundant "image"[3] that rises before them, not subjectively but objectively, at every moment. The Church and the world live historically in relation to this "image", which is an

[3] This image must at the same time remain "place-less" (u-topic) for all temporal and historical thinking.

image of the "Christ who comes again", while God's
Spirit seeks a comprehensive answer from the whole
of creation to God's loving Word in Christ and helps
give birth to this answer through the most intense
labor pains (Rom 8:19–27); God's love from below
sighs for God's love from above, until the miracle
of love brings about their perfect nuptial union (Rev
21:9f.).

b. But one could raise a weighty objection to gathering the whole "truth of revelation" around the
theme of divine love. Isn't judgment, at every point
in the Old Covenant, always the counterpart to love?
A "judgment without mercy" (James 2:13) falls over
all, not only those outside the narrow bounds of
God's heritage, Israel, but even those within who re-
sist the divine flame of jealous love that elects whom
it will. Is not Israel itself torn in two in a horrify-
ing way and placed between Gerizim and Ebal, the
mountain of promise and the mountain of damnation (Deut 27–28)? Is it not only a "remnant" of
Israel that is saved, while it is useless for the rest to
implore (Jer 7:16; 11:14; 14:11)? Jesus proclaims his
message of love in relation to this first Jerusalem, ir-
remediably condemned to the unquenchable fire of
God's wrath (Jer 7:20), and he does not do so without opening up even more horrible abysses than were
ever foreseeable by the Old Testament. There, being
blessed or happy, like being cursed and lost, could

have a meaning only in temporal terms; as long as heaven (Heb 11:40) was not open, there could not be a hell, (but only a predecessor to both: Hades, Sheol). It is only when that heaven has been opened that eternal hell opens up for the first time. The words are there; they cannot be overlooked and they cannot be hushed up. And the Spirit, the Consoler, will bring the world to understand that there is such a thing as sin, justice, and judgment (Jn 16:8). Whatever is found to be united with the powers of evil, with temptation and Babylon's destruction of love, will be thrown down together into the pit of fire with the great Babel and the creatures of the abyss, in order to be punished there day and night for all eternity. "This is the second death. If anyone's name was not found written in the Book of Life, he was thrown into the lake of fire" (Rev 20:9-10, 14-15; 21:8).

The ultimate abysses of man's freedom to oppose God open up at the place where God, in the freedom of his love, makes the decision to descend kenotically all the way into the forsakenness of the world. With his descent, he reveals this forsakenness: to himself, insofar as he wants to experience abandonment by God, and to the world, which only now measures the entire breadth of its own freedom to oppose God against the dimensions of God's love. From this point on, it becomes possible to sound out "the depths of Satan" (Rev 2:24). From this point on, true, deliberate atheism becomes possible for the very first time, since, prior to this, without a genuine concept of God, there could be no true atheism. God's making himself vulnerable in unshielded freedom yanked man from the shell of an all-embracing, divine-cosmic Logos and placed him in the nakedness of his own freedom in relation to God, a freedom that points to the Absolute. The Old Testament had been, in this regard, a long and strenuous training period: everything rests on the bilaterally free consent to the mutual Covenant; man can withdraw from it, but so can God, and only when this possibility is thought through and lived through in all of its consequences can the other possibility be affirmed, the possibility that far surpasses the first, namely, that, though God can reject and will reject, in the end, in eternity, he will save: "I have loved you with everlasting love" (Jer 31:3). Therefore, after all of the definitive rejections, the whole of Israel will be definitively saved (Rom 11:26).

The biblical language of the Old and New Covenants is prophetic language, the language of decision. There is a formal unity to the language in both the Old and New Testaments, that is, it is the articulation of a Covenant, and in fashioning this Covenant (since it is a Covenant between the God of love and man, who is always ready to abuse this love), the language must always necessarily present both objective possibilities. While the speculative theology

of the Patristic period and the Middle Ages system-
atized this prophetic ambivalence into a cosmology
(and doing so blunted the nub of the words), the
anthropological theology of modernity centered this
ambivalence around human existence and therefore
diluted it in part with psychological and pedagogical categories, in part with existential and logical (dialectical) categories. But in truth, the opening of the
flaming abyss of God's wrath depends on the opening
of the fiery abyss of divine love, which poured itself
out in the Heart that hung broken on the Cross and
in the descent into the shadows on Holy Saturday.
The supreme threat—coming from God the Father,
who as it were gives sinners his supreme love, God
the Son—swathes the broken heart like a sheltering cloak; it is a threat not to abuse this supreme
gift, because, behind it, there is no greater love to
call upon and to turn to (Heb 6:4–8; 10:26–31).
And once again, the Spirit of Love cannot teach the
Cross to the world in any other way than by disclos-
ing the full depths of the guilt that the world bears,
a guilt that comes to light on the Cross and is the
only thing that makes the Cross intelligible. Indeed,
it is in the God-forsakenness of the Crucified One
that we come to see what we have been redeemed
and saved from: the definitive loss of God, a loss
we could never have spared ourselves through any
of our own efforts outside of grace.

But the insight we gain through the Cross can

never bring us beyond the Cross: the moment we see our sins objectified before us on the Cross, it becomes all the more impossible to leave the One who died for us to his fate; so loveless a thought reveals our whole evil heart to us, love awakens fear in us, and the terrifying reality of being left behind by God (which is timeless as far as the one abandoned is concerned) shows us vividly that hell is no pedagogical threat, it is no mere "possibility". Instead, it is the reality that the God-forsaken one experienced in an eminent way because no one can even approximately experience the abandonment by God as horribly as the Son, who shares the same essence with the Father for all eternity.

Thus, both of our eternal lots lie together in his hand: precisely because he is our grace, he is also our judgment; he is our judge and at the same time our redeemer. As Christians, we know that the sins committed in the face of acknowledged love weigh imponderably more heavily than those committed in ignorance; this is why every standard of measurement for our attempts at loving God has been taken away, every systematic oversight over the outcome of our judgment, as well as the judgment of our neighbor and of the world. In the place of any such system—whether it be one that *knows* "cosmologically" that, in Christ's judgment, a certain number will enter into heaven and a certain number will enter into hell, or one that *knows* "anthropologically" that the threat of hell can be meant only as a pedagogical aid and that "everything" will ultimately turn out well—the Christian is entrusted with something far more valuable: Christian hope.

This hope is to be clearly distinguished from purely human hope, since it cannot be described in terms of uncertainty or calculations of probability, but like faith participates in the unconditionality and universality of love ("love believes all things and hopes all things" [1 Cor 13:7]) and thereby leaps over its own shadow ("hoping against all hope" [Rom 4:18]). As a spiritual and not merely instinctive act of the human being, it remains a paradox that reason cannot resolve and becomes understandable only when we take it seriously as a modality of love, at least as the beginnings of a love modeled on God (a "supernatural" love). Doing so, we come to see it as the only attitude that can be justified and therefore the only attitude that can be permitted for the one living by the sign of the Son of Man, which will "appear in the clouds" (Mt 24:30; Rev 1:7) and will be God's final "Word" to the world, after heaven and earth have passed away (Mt 24:35).

We are therefore not required to bring a systematically conceived hell into harmony with the love of God and make it credible,[4] or indeed to justify it

---

[4] As we read in Dante's *Inferno*: "Divine Power made me, / Highest Wisdom, and Primal Love" (canto 3, ll. 5–6).

conceptually as love (and not perhaps merely as the revelation of self-glorifying divine justice), because no such system could be constructed out of a possible "knowledge" apart from or beyond love and at the same time related to it. We are required only not to let go of love, the love that believes and hopes and through both is suspended in the air so that its Christian wings may grow. Soaring in the air, I also necessarily experience the abyss below, which is only part of my own flight. Similarly, I can speak of hell only in relation to myself, precisely because I can never imagine the possible damnation of another as more likely than my own.

A love that failed to recognize the infinite distance of reverential fear before the majesty of God's love on the Cross would have every reason to doubt itself, so too would any love that no longer contained any fear of judgment. Perhaps this love would have claimed perfection for itself in light of 1 John 4:17–18, but if it did so it would have failed to take seriously the disturbance in Jesus' soul and his sweating of blood before the Passion (Jn 11:33, 38; 12:27; 13:21; Lk 22:44). As one who is troubled, Jesus can, in love, console the apostles who are also troubled (Jn 14:1), and in whose midst the traitor sits. The Redeemer in his anxiety no longer desired or was able to make a distinction between his own innocence and the foreign guilt of those for whom he atoned; likewise, the man who in the trial of love

joins God's love in suffering for both his own guilt
and that of the world will no longer be able to distinguish clearly what causes his anguish: the only
thing clear is that he has every reason to be anxious
for himself.

And thus whoever simply refuses to shut his eyes
to the abyss of hatred, despair, and depravity that
can be seen in the life of men on earth, and thus
who refuses to close himself off from reality, will
find it difficult to contrive his own escape from this
damnation through a purely individualistic conception of salvation, and to abandon everyone else to
the grinding wheels of hell. Just as God so loved the
world that he completely handed over his Son for
its sake, so too the one whom God has loved will
want to save himself only in conjunction with those
who have been created with him, and he will not
reject the share of penitential suffering that has been
given him for the sake of the whole. He will do so
in Christian hope, the hope for the salvation of all
men, which is permitted to Christians alone. Thus,
the Church is strictly enjoined to pray "for *all* men"
(and as a result of which to see her prayer in this
respect as meaningful and effective); and it is "good
and it is acceptable in the sight of God our Savior,
who desires *all* men to be saved . . . , for there is one
God, and there is one mediator between God and
men, the man Christ Jesus, who gave himself over
as a ransom for *all*" (1 Tim 2:1–6), who, raised up

on the Cross, "will draw *all* men to himself" (Jn
12:32), because he has received there the "power
over *all* flesh" (Jn 17:2), in order to be "a Savior
of *all* men" (1 Tim 4:10), "in order to take away
the sins of *all*" (Heb 9:28); "for the grace of God
has appeared for the salvation of *all* men" (Tit 2:11),
which is why the Church "looks to the advantage
of *all* men, in order that they may be saved" (1 Cor
10:33). This is why Paul (Rom 5:15–21) can say that
the balance between sin and grace, fear and hope,
damnation and redemption, and Adam and Christ
has been tilted in the favor of grace, and indeed so
much so that (in relation to redemption) the mountain of sin stands before an inconceivable superabundance of redemption: not only have all been doomed
to (the first and the second) death in Adam, while all
have been freed from death in Christ, but the sins of
all, which assault the innocent one and culminate in
God's murder, have brought an inexhaustible wealth
of absolution down upon *all*. Thus: "God has con-
signed *all* men to disobedience, that he may have
mercy upon *all*" (Rom 11:32).

7. Love as Justification and Faith

The sign of Christ is legible only if we read his human love and self-gift unto death as the manifestation of absolute love. Seeing this relationship would prevent us from putting his humanity on a pedestal, making him a hero or superhuman demigod (as ancient Gnosticism and Arianism did, and as a certain well-meaning but unenlightened Christology has a tendency to do even today) and thereby obscuring the real manifestation of love. What most decisively draws our attention to Christ is not that he is more powerful than other human beings (that is, that he has an unheard-of knowledge and strength of will and other psychic or parapsychic powers, which would perhaps serve to explain his miracles), but that he seeks to be so "meek and humble of heart" (Mt 11:29) and therefore so "poor in spirit" (Mt 5:3) that absolute love might shine through his human love and become present in it. Indeed, such an attitude of love can ultimately be determined (conceived and carried out) only on the basis of this absolute love. Christ's act of creating space in himself for God is not self-mastery, but is itself already obedience, an obedience willing to take on whatever task the "ever greater Father" gives. The task, however, consists in letting the sins of the world into the same space he had allowed the Father to fill, and to do so out of the love that God also fills, as the "Lamb of God who takes away the sins of the world" (Jn 1:29), and therefore takes away mine.

It is always the dogma of the removal of guilt through representative substitution that shows most decisively whether an approach is merely anthropologically or truly christologically (that is, theologically) centered. Without this dogma, it always remains possible to interpret everything in rational terms as an expression of human possibility, no matter how much historical mediation one wishes to build in. Our inability to resolve this dogma into gnosis is the true scandal; it is a signal and a warning that this is where genuine faith begins. For it is precisely here, in this deed, that genuine divine love begins and ends, a love that overwhelms us and exceeds all capacity to think it—and thereby becomes completely evident *as* love. Ultimately, there can be absolute faith *only* in this deed, because only such a deed, *if* it should happen, is absolute love, love as *the* absolute, as the ungraspable epitome of the wholly-other God: "We believe the love God has for us" (1 Jn 4:16).

If this is true, then "the life I now live in the flesh I live by faith in the Son of God, who loved *me* and gave himself for *me*" (Gal 2:20). Faith, in this case, means the fundamental response to the love that has offered itself up for me. A response that always comes too late because the deed God carried out in Christ, the bearing away of my sins, has already taken place, before any response was possible, before a response could even be considered. Occurring thus in pure gratuity, the deed demonstrates pure and absolute love: "God shows his love for us in that while we were yet sinners Christ died for us. . . . While we were enemies we were reconciled to God by the death of his Son" (Rom 5:8, 10). How can an enemy be reconciled while he is still an enemy? Apparently, with God, such a thing is possible; and from this unheard-of idea, St. Paul infers that, after our justification through Christ's death, which has made us his reconciled friends, we will all the more certainly have peace with God through his life (Rom 9–10).

It thus becomes clear that faith is ordered primarily to the inconceivability of God's love, which surpasses us and anticipates us. This is the sole object, the sole *daß* (Martin Buber), of faith, as the Christian creed expresses it. Love alone is credible; nothing else can be believed, and nothing else ought to be believed. This is the achievement, the "work" of faith: to recognize this absolute *prius*, which nothing else can surpass; to believe that there is such a thing as love, absolute love, and that there is nothing higher or greater than it; to believe against all the evidence of experience ("*credere contra fidem*" like "*sperare contra spem*"), against every "rational" concept of God, which thinks of him in terms of impassibility or, at best, totally pure goodness, but not in terms of this inconceivable and senseless act of love.

The first thing that must strike a non-Christian about the Christian's faith is that it obviously presumes far too much. It is too good to be true: the mystery of being, revealed as absolute love, condescending to wash his creatures' feet, and even their souls, taking upon himself all the confusion of guilt, all the God-directed hatred, all the accusations showered upon him with cudgels, all the disbelief that arrogantly covers up what he had revealed, all the mocking hostility that once and for all nailed down his inconceivable movement of self-abasement—in order to pardon his creature, before himself and the world. This is truly too much from the Good; nothing in the world would justify such a metaphysics, and therefore it cannot be justified by that individual sign called "Jesus of Nazareth", which has so little historical evidence and is so difficult to decipher. To build such an extravagant building on such a fragile foundation would overstep all the limits of reason. And why not, instead, remain (like Martin Buber) with a humanly and ecumenically interpreted Old Testament and its "open" and undogmatic faith? In this sphere, theological speech becomes impossible to distinguish from anthropological speech, and this

"open faith" converges with Jaspers' "open reason".
But in this case we are still dealing with "wisdom"
—and we have thus succeeded once again: to escape
from the absolute sign of the scandal of the Cross.

Once a person learns to read the signs of love
and thus to believe it, love leads him into the open
field wherein he himself can love. If the prodigal
son had not believed that the father's love was already there waiting for him, he would not have been
able to make the journey home—even if his father's
love welcomes him in a way he never would have
dreamed of. The decisive thing is that the sinner has
heard of a love that could be, and really is, there for
him; he is not the one who has to bring himself into
line with God; God has always already seen in him,
the loveless sinner, a beloved child and has looked
upon him and conferred dignity upon him in the
light of this love.

No one can resolve this mystery into dry concepts
and explain how it is that God no longer sees my
guilt in me, but only in his beloved Son, who bears
it for me; or how God sees this guilt transformed
through the suffering of love and loves me because
I am the one for whom his Son has suffered in love.
But the way God, the lover, sees us is in fact the
way we *are* in reality—for God, this is the absolute
and irrevocable truth. This is why there can be no
talk of "merely forensic" justification; the theory is
valid only in the sense that, through God's creative

and transformative love, we become what he takes us to be in the light of Christ. One can attempt to break down the psychological or "theological" stages of the infinitely mysterious process by which our being represented in Christ becomes Christ's being represented in us, the process by which grace transforms Christ's love for the Father and for us into our response to love, but these will never reflect anything but fragments of the process. The deeper the rays of God's justifying love penetrate into our being as "sanctification", the more it unconditionally strengthens and evokes our freedom for love. In a sort of "primordial generation", it calls forth in us a response to love, and though it remains stammering and inchoate in us, the response acquires, through the mediation of the Son's abundant love (and therefore through total faith in him), its own fullness and suitability. For there exists a perfect correspondence between divine and human love in the Son, and he confers this correspondence (as we showed above) upon the Church as a perfectly valid measure, so that she can give birth to him, the Son, and all of his brothers (Rev 12:17) in a human way. We have been incorporated into this "perfect measure" (Eph 4:13), and therefore our deficiencies have always already been overcome and compensated for, so that, out of faith, we can bring ever more fully to life in Christian activity that which God's holy grace has always already allowed us to be in his eyes.

The fact that the horizon of the love given to us always lies above and before us, and that the disparity can never be eliminated in this life, at the same time justifies everything presented as the "dogmatic" aspect of faith: if love, which is truth, always remains infinitely more than we can achieve—not as a nonexisting idea, but rather as complete reality (in Christ and in his immaculate bride, the Church), which as such enables us in fact to strive for it— then our self-gift in faith to an ever-greater love is always necessarily at the same time a self-gift of faith to its ever-greater truth. By the same token, because it is pure love, we are unable to achieve "insight" into it in a gnostic manner with the resources of our own reason; an encounter with pure love and its gift for us remains the pure, inconceivable miracle. The individual "mysteries", which are "presented as things to be believed", are nothing more than conditions of possibility for the perception of love in Christ: the Father (as the Personal Other) is the one who sends, so that the kenotic and obediential character of the Son's love never be lost from view; the Spirit is the one who is breathed forth, so that not only the freedom and fruitfulness be revealed, but also the shared mutuality, the witness and glorification character, the pure in-itselfness of the love beyond the Logos; the essential identity of the three "Persons" in the Godhead is alone what guarantees the absolute name of Love to God and definitively rescues love—to the joy of those who believe in love—from the clutches of prying reason,[1] giving "strength" to those "in whose hearts Christ dwells . . . being rooted and grounded in love, . . . that they may know the love of Christ which far surpasses all knowledge" (Eph 3:17–19).

[1] This is not to deny the possibility of dogmatic theology as the "logical interpretation" of God's kenosis of love. Indeed, it is even necessary both for preaching and for the Church's own contemplative reflection—granted, however, that the mystery of love remains at the center, around which all attempts to conceptualize it turn. The Spirit of holiness and love is also the Spirit of wisdom and knowledge about love; and they are in fact one and the same Spirit: "Truth and love are inseparable wings—for truth cannot fly without love—and love cannot hover without truth" (Ephrem, *Hymnen Vom Glauben*, 20, ed. Beck [1955], 59–60).

8. Love as Deed

Love desires no recompense other than to be loved in return; and thus God desires nothing in return for his love for us other than our love. "Let us not love in word or speech, but in deed [ἔργον] and in truth" (1 Jn 3:18). To understand this deed of love primarily, not to say exclusively, as something passed on apostolically from man to man, would be to instrumentalize the revelation of absolute love, wholly reducing it to a means or impulse directed to a human end, rather than seeing it as personal and absolute itself. To center Christianity in anthropology and thus turn it into a pure ethics would be to eliminate its theo-logical dimension. Israel, which was not (and is not) apostolic, or at least not principally, must remain a warning in this respect: the jealous God, who makes a gift of himself in the covenant, desires in the first place nothing other than his partner's zealously faithful love—for him. Indeed, we must love absolute love and direct our love to the Lover, setting aside all other relative and competing objects of love. To the extent that we do not remain absolutely faithful to absolute love, these objects turn into idols. The bridegroom and the bride in the Song

of Songs have no children; they are everything and
sufficient for one another, and all their fruitfulness
lies enclosed within the circle of their mutual love:
hortus conclusus, fons signatus.

In the same way, every Christian "apostolate"
strays from love and becomes a rationalized siphon-
ing of love (cf. Judas' pseudo-charitable objection to
Mary's utterly "wasteful" *squandering* in Jn 12:3–8)
to the extent that absolute love does not receive a response that is likewise absolute and not directed to
any ulterior end. We call this response "worship"
(Jn 4:24; 9:38; Rev 14:7), the pure "thanks-giving"
that gives glory (Mt 15:36 and parallels, Rom 1:8,
etc.; 1 Thess 5:18; Rev 4:9); it is a response that
must be fashioned into a form that gathers up and
confers meaning upon one's entire existence (1 Cor
10:31; Col 3:17). Unconditional priority must be
accorded to the placing of oneself entirely at the disposal of divine love. Since it serves no ulterior purpose, this attitude of readiness cannot but appear useless in the eyes of the world, which is caught up in so
many urgent and reasonable occupations (Lk 10:42).
The ranking of the contemplative life over the active life outside Christianity, because it enables one
to achieve liberation through a particular gnosis and
praxis, corresponds within Christianity—and only at
this point—to the superiority of a life given purely
as an answer to God's self-giving love. This answer
is made in the faith that God's love, from which all
fruitfulness stems, will be powerful enough to pro-

duce all of the fruit pleasing to him in mankind and the world out of this single-hearted nuptial surrender. This is the essence of Carmel, and of every genuinely "contemplative" life in the Church. The word "contemplative" can be misinterpreted in a gnostic sense, but it means the life praised by Jesus, the life of Mary at his feet.

Prayer, both ecclesial and personal prayer, thus ranks higher than all action, not in the first place as a source of psychological energy ("refueling", as they say today), but as the act of worship and glorification that befits love, the act in which one makes the most fundamental attempt to answer with selflessness and thereby shows that one has understood the divine proclamation. It is as tragic as it is ridiculous to see Christians today giving up this fundamental priority —which is witnessed to by the entire Old and New Testament, by Jesus' life as much as by Paul's and John's theology—and seeking instead an immediate encounter with Christ in their neighbor, or even in purely worldly work and technological activity. Engaged in such work, they soon lose the capacity to see any distinction between worldly responsibility and Christian mission. Whoever does not come to know the face of God in contemplation will not recognize it in action, even when it reveals itself to him in the face of the oppressed and humiliated.

Moreover, the celebration of the Eucharist is itself an *anamnesis*, which means that it is contemplation in love and the communion of love with love;

and it is only from such a celebration that a Christian mission goes out into the world: "*Ite missa-missio est!*" For Paul's command to "pray without ceasing" (1 Thess 5:17) can be carried out in action, not primarily as a technique and training in the sense of the Eastern "Jesus prayer", but rather in analogy to the young man who carries alive and active in his heart a picture of his beloved even into those occupations that would take him away from her, or to the knight of the old romances who performed all of his deeds for the glorification of his lady. "Good intention" is a weak formulation for something much stronger, something that comes to expression in various Christian sayings: let the "glory of God be praised in all things" (Eph 1:6), so that "God be glorified in all things" (Benedict), let "everything happen for the greater glory of God" (Ignatius of Loyola).

This glorification occurs in the human act insofar as it is inspired by love and is ordered to love. Just as life gathers up and gives form to matter from the ground up, so too the "virtue" of love (*caritas forma virtutum* as the fundamental principle of all Christian ethics, whether from an Augustinian or a Thomistic perspective) gives definitive form and meaning to the natural, living "material" of the soul, which has been previously formed through the natural virtues. *Caritas* is any encounter with one's neighbor that, when seen from the point of view of God's judgment, can be interpreted as an encounter in absolute love, that is, in the love of God as it has been made known in Christ. The issue here is one of interpretation, of making visible all of the presuppositions or consequences implied in our encounter with our neighbor when illuminated by the fire of judgment. This interpretation is not a "reading into", but is absolutely objective, as the verdict of judgment shows: "Truly, I say to you, whatever [of these acts of love] you did [or failed to do] to the least of these brethren, you did [or failed to do] to me" (Mt 25:40, 45). This verdict elicits the shock of disbelief as much from those who have done these acts as from those who have not ("When, Lord, did we see thee hungry . . . and thirsty . . . and as a stranger . . . and naked and sick and in prison?"). For no one but Christ alone succeeds in directing his action entirely to Christ; and thus, if we live in loving faith, our ethical standard is in the end taken from our hands and placed in the love of God.

But what is implicated in the transaction of the one acting in faith and the object of this deed, that is, the "neighbor", is nothing less than revelation itself, and, with it, the whole *network of dogmas*. Dogmatic theology is the articulation of the conditions of possibility of Christian action in the light of revelation —which we can sketch out only in broad strokes in the present context. There is not a single proposition of dogma that Christian action can dispense with, even if the one acting does not have explicit knowledge of it or, though he knows it, does not take notice of it in relation to the existential situation of the encounter. Christian action is above all a secondary reaction to the primary action of God toward man ("I forgave you all your debt, . . . and should not you have had mercy on your fellow servant?" Mt 18:32–33). If God's prior action were not presupposed, our deed would have to take its measure from the identity of human nature, from a consideration of the inevitable limitations that arise from living in community, and from equalizing the interests of the I and the Thou (*suum cuique*), if not also from the superiority of the I, who deigns to forgive, over the Thou, who is inwardly unworthy of this magnanimity—which is quite a dubious situation from an ethical perspective.

Only by presupposing God's prior and inconceivable forgiveness can the limitations of human good will be transcended, and only thus can the danger of human pride be avoided: through God's love, I am first of all one who has been humbled, for my "entire debt" had first to be forgiven, and my own secondary act of forgiveness is merely an echo; indeed, it is nothing but an act of simple obedience and not at all something proceeding from my own sovereign will. Limitations thus fall away: because God forgave me while I was still his enemy (Rom 5:10), I must also forgive my fellow men even while they are enemies (Mt 5:43–48); because God has given

to me without counting the costs, to the point of
wholly losing himself (Mt 27:46), I must surrender
any worldly calculation of the relationship between
almsgiving and compensation (Mt 6:1–4; 6:19–34);
the standard that God lays down becomes the standard that I must lay down, and thus the standard by
which I myself am measured. This is not a principle of "mere justice", but the logic of absolute love.
Once again, it is the unconditionality of this love,
which is done to us and which we must therefore allow to be done to others, that contains "fear" within
itself.

Since the believer's action is rooted in God's prior
act, he cannot help at the same time directing his action toward it. In other words, his action is essentially eschatological, or (since that word has been
overburdened) *parousial*. He acts in view of this essential tenet of Christian faith, namely, that Christ
will come again in the "glory" of the revealed love
that judges and rectifies all things at the (timeless)
end of the chain of all temporal events. Action always proceeds forward, action that arises from the
absolute proceeds toward the absolute future, which
lies within and beyond the relative history of the
world (Paul Schütz).[1] For this reason, the "least"

---

[1] In this sense, God himself, as creator and redeemer, thinks and
acts in a progressive way, looking to the definitive image that "hovers
before" him: *Tales nos amat Deus quales* futuri *sumus ipsius dono, non
quales sumus nostro merito* [God loves us, not such as we are by our

encounter, or the encounter with the "least of these brethren", has a place in the seriousness of judgment. If Christ has borne this least one and taken away his guilt, then I have to see him, through my faith in love, as he looks in the eyes of my Father in heaven; this image alone is true, and the one that I have, which seems so clear to me, is false. The Christian encounters Christ *in* his neighbor, not beyond him or above him; and only in this way does the encounter correspond to the incarnate and suffering love of the one who calls himself "Son of God" without the article (Jn 5:27), and who is the nearest to us in all those who are near.

The duality between "any particular man" and "Son of Man" in the encounter can be resolved in faith only by seeing human sin where it truly belongs, in the Son of Man, who "was made to be sin, so that in him we might become the righteousness of God" (2 Cor 5:21), and thus by seeing Christ's righteousness in this man himself, as the truth that has been given to him and toward which his existence is ordered. In other words, this twofold unity is in fact to be read "through the Cross". But when we read it thus, the Cross eliminates guilt by transforming it, through love, into love. The eyes required to see my neighbor in this way are given to me only

merit, but such as we will be by his own gift] (Prosper, in the 2nd Council of Orange, c. 12, Denz., 185).

in faith, in the faith that I myself live in God only because Christ died for my sake, a fact that therefore obliges me to interpret all things according to what this love demands.

Justification in faith is therefore the presupposition for any and every Christian encounter, both for me and for the Thou; it follows that the encounter contains implicitly everything that is objectively implied in justification. Thus, as remarked above, it implies the attitude of blind obedience, which sees only the image of Christ shining in the other, because it transcends all of its own (psychological) evidence. Thus, it also implies prayer, since every existential conversation I have with the Thou presupposes that both of us are already included within the Word of God and therefore within the triune conversation of love. This trinitarian conversation is the conversation the incarnate Son has with the Father, wherein the immeasurable gulf between the world as it is and as it ought to be for God, is endured to the end, answered for, and—in the ultimate existential engagement of the Word of God —bridged over. It is only by virtue of this conversation, by virtue of this deepest of all Christian mysteries, that the divergence of perspective in heaven and on earth can be brought into unity—through the Son's indifference with respect to the Father's will and in the "deference" of the Father with respect to the Son's will (Jn 17:24). It is only by virtue

of this conversation that we do not need to break off
our human concern for our neighbor because of dis-
couragement, because "nothing more can be done".
By leaving everything in God's hands, the love that
bears all things carries us further; it achieves more
in the extreme suffering of not "being able to go
on any further" than in potent, self-assured action.
This is why Thérèse of Lisieux can describe life in
Carmel as the most apostolically fruitful life.

To keep one's eyes fixed on the love of Christ
does not, however, mean that one overlooks one's
neighbor's mistakes; the Samaritan had to see the
wounds he was supposed to tend to (as Francis de
Sales put it, *voir sans regarder*). A teacher has to be
aware of the child's lack of knowledge and ability in
order to carry out his task; similarly, the Christian
has to look on everything in the world that stands
against God with "realistic" vision (indeed, an insight into the depth of this resistance to God is avail-
able only to the Christian, in the light of the Cross),
and he at the same time has to see it only in relation
to the Cross, in which the world has already been
conquered (Jn 12:31; 16:33).

Christian action is therefore a being taken up into
God's action through grace, being taken up into
God's love so that one can love with him. It is only
here that (Christian) *knowledge about God* becomes
possible, for "he who does not love, does not know
God; for God is love" (1 Jn 4:8). Love, in this con-

text, means unconditional commitment, which implicitly (that is, when necessary) includes a willingness to go all the way to one's death: "Greater love has no man than this, that a man lay down his life for his friends" (Jn 15:13). "By this we know love, that he laid down his life for us; and we ought to lay down our lives for the brethren" (1 Jn 3:16). This is the fundamental law for all Christian ethics, and even for all Christian knowledge: to carry out one's action in conjunction with what has already been done in its fullness, and therefore to bring about and perfect that which has already been brought about and perfected, since it is only in this way that what is revealed in itself becomes revealed also to us: "Beloved, if God so loved us, we ought also to love one another. No man has ever seen God; [but] if we love one another, then God abides in us and his love is perfected in us" (τετελειωμένη, 1 Jn 4:11–12). Here it becomes clear why John—in contrast to the synoptic Gospels' apparently one-sided emphasis on the "love of one's enemies" that streams forth into the loveless void—emphasizes the reciprocity of love so strongly and almost reductively (Jn 13:34–35; 15:12–13, 17); this is the only way to make visible the trinitarian foundation of Christian love. Even John's inclusion of the enemy and his darkness within the fold of the eucharistic community of love (Jn 13:21–30) simply exhibits this principle in the most extreme case.

Above, we showed the extent to which the dogmas of *ecclesiology and mariology* form part of the fundamental figure of revelation; they arise here once again as conditions of possibility of Christian action. We do not represent the proper measure of absolute love in human form to the world as isolated individuals. We do not have a monopoly on its spirit; we are merely failing members of a comprehensive whole who have been allowed to share in this spirit. Whatever is impure and fallible in us becomes immaculate and infallible in the innermost core of this whole. Our obedience of faith in relation to this absolute norm is embodied in our relationship to the Church (who is the Lord's Bride and our Mother). As members, we participate in the humility of the handmaid, in her perfect obedience to the Lord, to the extent that we are obedient as parts to her whole. But because this obedience is identical in essence with her loving obedience to the Lord, she does not represent an intermediary between us and Christ. Instead, she is an essential step in the process of our integration on the way to the Parousia. The Church's sacraments are the immediate articulation of the Bridegroom's love for his Bride; the recipient of this love is always the individual believer who stands immediately within the parish community; the deacon/servant who administers the sacraments (or approves them, in the case of marriage) has the role of making these sacraments immediately present in society, but at the same time, as we have already shown, he is also the one who represents the authoritative majesty that transcends individuality, as well as the normative ("legitimate") validity of God's love.

It corresponds to the essence of the Church that not only should the canonical standard be established at the level of the "purity without blemish" of the absolutely normative Bride-Bridegroom relationship (the mariology and ecclesiology of Ephesians 5:27), but also at the level of every approximation of this purity in those who deserved to be raised up ("canonized") as canons for the believer's human life in the love of the Church. The people who live entirely for love are not merely "moral examples" of Christian action, but, because they have handed themselves over to the fruitful love of the Redeemer, they are also our intercessors and chosen helpers. In the place that has been designated for them, however, they do no more than point to the total reciprocal integration of the deeds of all those who love; in the infinite, their lives and deeds open up to one another and mutually interpenetrate (the "communion of saints"). From this perspective, every Christian encounter is an event within this community, and there is always a responsibility (*missio*), given as much by Christ as by the Church, to enter every situation as a representative of the whole and of the comprehensive idea of love. This is the Christian version of the categorical imperative, by virtue of which absolute love, as a "duty" that transcends every individual "inclination", is elevated and ordered to itself, with the implacability of the Cross of Jesus Christ, and with the severity and burning flame of the living Christ himself, who seeks to set the whole of world history aflame with the fire of his love: "His eyes were like a flame of fire, his feet were like burnished bronze, refined as in a furnace, and his voice was like the sound of many waters, . . . from his mouth issued a sharp, two-edged sword, and his face was like the sun shining in full strength. When I saw him, I fell at his feet as though dead" (Rev 1:14–17). The Beloved Apostle's vision already perfectly reflects the consuming fire of the Gospel itself, which contains and surpasses all of the ardor of the Old Testament combined. And what burns most searingly here is that the absolute impatience of divine love conceals itself in the absolute humility and poverty of the heart (just as the storm of Sinai is concealed in the quiet whisper of Mount Horeb), precisely so that, when it does burst forth, it is all the more overwhelming.

The *saints* experienced something of the heat of this categorical imperative; we can see it in their lives and actions. It is in them that Christian love becomes credible; they are the poor sinners' guiding stars. But every one of them wishes to point completely away from himself and toward love. Wherever the gap between absolute love and the lovers pointing to it diminishes through some sort of "identity"—in terms of a pietistic, or mystical, or spiritual, or Joachimite theology (for example, when Francis, or even simply the priest, is taken to be an "alter Christus", and so forth)—the love revealed by the Bible immediately loses its credibility. In this case, the decisively Christian element would be threatened or even eclipsed by the general, anthropological element. Likewise, the saints' love would lie like a flashy mantle over their fully developed "religious personality"; they would once again be seeking their own glory, however surreptitiously, and they would be coming in their own name (Jn 5:41f.); the "eternal in man" (Scheler) would sparkle as an illuminated background, always on the verge of changing immediately into the "eternal man" (as Scheler shows at the end of his life).

But the genuine saints desired nothing but the greater glory of God's love; this alone is the condition of possibility of what they do. A person would contradict them outright if, thinking he knows better, he were to interpret their deeds as means of self-glorification. The saints are lost in the depths of God; they are hidden in him. Their perfection grows not around the center of their ego, but solely around the center of God, whose inconceivable and incalculable grace it is to make his creature freer in himself and for himself to the extent that he becomes freer for God alone. We can resolve this paradox only if we understand, in the light of God's self-gift, that he is love, which is just as jealous as it is without envy, so that it can gather exclusively to itself just as much as it casts itself out to all.

The sole credibility of the Church Christ founded lies, as he himself says, in the saints, as those who sought to set all things on the love of Christ alone. It is in them that we can see what the "authentic" Church is, that is, what she is in her authenticity, while she is essentially obscured by sinners (as people who do not seriously believe in God's love) and turned into a useless enigma, which as such deservedly provokes contradiction and blasphemy (Rom 2:24). Christ's apologetic, by contrast, can be summarized in the sentence: "By this all men will know that you are my disciples, if you have love for one another" (Jn 13:35). This, however, means demonstrating the truth of dogma: "I in them, and thou in me, that they may be perfectly one, so that the world may know that thou hast sent me and hast loved them even as thou hast loved me" (Jn 17:23). Love as deed: a deed that is as genuinely human (with a heavy emphasis on corporal works of mercy) as it is therefore genuinely divine (because it is granted by God's patience and humility), and thus a deed that becomes effectively present through everything that happens in the Church (in the preaching and the Mass and the sacraments and the organization and canon law)—this is the "proof of spirit and power".

It is only at this point, concluding with a flourish, that one can speak about the ultimate mystery of love. This is the *magnum mysterium* of the "one flesh" (Eph 5:31), as being "one in spirit" (1 Cor 6:17), as "one bread, one body" (1 Cor 10:17). A mystery of unspeakable unity, "no longer living for oneself" (2 Cor 5:15), but henceforward living only for the One who loves, indeed, "no longer do I live, but Christ lives in me" (Gal 2:20), "God himself shines in our hearts" (2 Cor 4:6). A reciprocal indwelling that lies beyond all imagination, proceeding from the perception of the "unveiled vision of the glory [of love] of the Lord" to an "ever more glorious reflection through the transformation into the same image, which the Lord works through the power of the Spirit" (2 Cor 3:18).

9. Love as Form

But if love can be measured by nothing other than itself—neither by "works", for these are (at best) only an echo of love, nor by faith (insofar as faith, when schizophrenically severed from love, becomes a mere positing of the truth of something), nor by suffering, which can also occur against one's will, nor by sacrifice, which can be self-righteousness, nor, finally, by a form of subjective experience of God (mysticism), which can be in part something also granted to one who does not love, but only by love itself—then love appears as formless, transcending all creaturely determinateness and precisely for this reason a threat to it. One must first of all endure this apparent formlessness, for love is unconditional assent to and readiness for God's will, whether this will has expressed itself yet or not; love is an a priori Yes to whatever may come, whether it be the Cross, or being plunged into absolute abandonment, or being forgotten, or utter uselessness and meaninglessness. It is the Son's Yes to the Father, the Mother's Yes to the angel, because he carries God's Word, the Church's Yes, given in and with all her members, to her Lord's sovereign will: "If it is my will . . . , what is that to you?" (Jn 21:22, 23). This love is "the mind of the Church", which the Church possesses subjectively in relation to Christ, and therefore objectively as a norm for the mind of her members.

But, as the "seed of God" (1 Jn 3:9), God's love implants itself into this threefold absolute openness of love as *fiat*, giving it determination and form; it is the Father's "will", "pleasure", "plan", "intention", "decision", "predetermination" (Eph 1:1–11), in which the Son's mission takes form. This form, then, informs the Church's mission, which, in turn, informs the Christian's mission and ultimately, in the service of God's comprehensive plan, informs the entire structure of creation with its countless individual structures in space and time. Nature's forms spring forth from creation, rising up and opening themselves in spirit and love to the infinity of fructifying grace; they thus receive from above their ultimate form [*Gestalt*], which recasts everything natural and reorders it.[1] The archetype of this process is the way in which the human nature of Christ points

[1] "Ego in tempora dissilui, . . . donec in Te confluam purgatus et liquidus igne amoris Tui. Et stabo atque consolidabor in Te, in forma mea" (Augustine, *Confessiones*, XI, chaps. 29 and 30). ["But I am scattered in times whose order I do not understand . . . until that day when, purified and molten by the fire of your love, I flow together to merge into you. Then shall I find stability and solidity in you, in your truth which imparts form to me", trans. Henry Chadwick (Oxford: Oxford University Press, 1991), 244.]

"ek-statically" toward his divine Person and, in fact, draws its existence from this Person. The Father's mission gives form, not only to his office and destiny as redeemer, down to its most insignificant details, but also gives form to the essential traits of his individual nature. He takes on a human existence in order to sacrifice it to God for all men and for the world as a whole, in order to unite God and the world in this liquidation [*Verflüßigung*] of himself, in order to receive the sacrificed nature (and thus the world) transformed and eternalized in the Resurrection, and in order to lay this same nature (and thus the world) eternally into the Father's hands.

This is the form, and it is into this form that Christ was baptized: one's baptism "into Jesus' death" is being "buried therefore with him by baptism into death, so that as Christ was raised from the dead by the glory of the Father, we too might walk in newness of life" (Rom 6:3–4). This new life can be nothing other than Christ's eternal life, to which there is no other access other than through the perfect *fiat*. This *fiat* is thus given in an objective, sacramental way in baptism; it is pronounced by the Mother-Church in a representative way on behalf of every baptized child and must then be fundamentally ratified by this child in a lifelong, stuttering attempt to approximate it existentially. The fundamental ratification is faith, which has the form of genuine faith only when it concedes all justice to God a priori and without conditions, in spite of all of reason's complaints that it itself knows better. This stuttering is love's attempt, step by step, to realize the truth of this fundamental surrender of oneself to God. Freedom from the compulsion of sin is freedom to serve God (Rom 6:12–14), a service wherein man stands in the nakedness of death awaiting his new form from God as a baptismal gown: "For as many of you as were baptized into Christ have put on Christ" (Gal 3:27), "and put on the new nature, created after the likeness of God in true righteousness and holiness" (Eph 4:24), and therefore put on the form of Christ's life, "put on then, as God's chosen ones, holy and beloved, compassion, kindness, lowliness, meekness, and patience, forbearing one another and, if one has a complaint against another, forgiving each other; as the Lord has forgiven you, so you also must forgive. And above all these put on love, which binds everything together in perfect harmony" (Col 3:12–14).

This love, which brings to ultimate perfection—in the double sense of an ultimate opening up to the infinite and a gathering together into a conclusion—is necessarily form-giving. As the *ultima forma*, it is what gives meaning to all the anticipatory stages and processes of integration. Love, however, as the last passage cited clearly indicates, is not just any love, but precisely the love of Christ, the love of the new and eternal Covenant: Love *as* "heartfelt compassion", as "kind, receptive openness", "an attitude of lowliness", "a meekness that does not defend itself", "long-suffering patience", and thus the winning over, the enduring of one's unendurable brothers, and forgiving them because God has forgiven— in short the sort of "virtue" that has already received its defining character from the "perfect bond".

This love is first of all the goal of the entire Old Testament education of man, which sought to conform man inwardly to God. This process of education necessarily passed through the spheres of natural and worldly virtues, which were taken up and ordered to the final form. But this occurred in such a way that the spheres were in the meantime only inspired with an impetus to move beyond themselves. A person thus knew (through faith in the God who leads) only that he must continue to transcend toward some goal, but without having any vision of the final form itself. We see this in the sphere of politics, where Israel attacked its (and God's) enemies in the name of the almighty God Yahweh, at first with earthly power, waging war to the point of ruthless devastation; we see it, too, in the sphere of social ethics, wherein the rights of the poor, the disenfranchised, and the oppressed were championed in a fundamental way from the beginning and ever more insistently by the prophets; and we see it in the sphere of individual ethics, where the individual was trained to renounce any immediate vision or possession and to adopt a higher perspective, wherein God's mills of justice grind slowly, high above human beings.

All this possesses its truth only within a dynamic

movement toward Christ's form of love—so much so that, while the Church offers her support to everything in the political, social, and ethical projects of the post-Christian world that can be ordered toward this love, she nevertheless herself clings obstinately to the point of perfection, "wishing to know nothing among you except Jesus Christ and him crucified" (1 Cor 2:2). It is thus not legitimate for the Church, under the pretext of sanctifying political power, to return to an Old Testament point of view, to seek to practice later New Testament love by means of earlier Old Testament power acquired through war. This is the integralists' approach, according to whom the expression *"In hoc signo vinces"* is to be interpreted as "in the sign of worldly failure you will achieve worldly success." It is not even possible—though admittedly this comes much closer to the New Testament—for the Church to absolutize the struggle for social justice, and thus to identify with it, the way Christian socialists do, with the intention afterward to lend it a Christian coloring. The preaching of social justice and work on its behalf must be informed by New Testament love from the ground up, as it always was with the apostles (2 Cor 8–9; 1 Jn 3:17; James 2:1–5, and so forth), and as Christ, the poorest of the poor, himself insisted, when he placed himself—that is, placed the absolute squandering of self in love—above a rational concern for the poor, for the proletariat (Jn 12:8). Only in this way is love of neighbor able to preserve its character as something ordered to the Absolute, to the Son of Man.

St. Paul himself always emphasized that the highest values of individual ethics are untenable without love. Love alone fulfills every law by being its exemplar (Rom 13:10; Gal 5:14); outside of love, the law is nothing but a negative safeguard against the sin that is taken for granted (1 Thess 1:8f.). Not even the faith that Abraham justified, not even the selling of all goods for the sake of the poor, which is what Jesus recommended for perfection, not to mention religious "knowledge", is "something" without love (1 Cor 13:1–3). Love alone leads us into the transcendence that brings perfection; love alone is the "more excellent way" (1 Cor 12:31), which thus also gives form to faith and hope (1 Cor 13:7). Everything in Scripture that is not itself love is a figure of love (Pascal).

The same relationship obtains between natural virtues and Christian love, whether one wishes to emphasize the more negative aspect of the relationship, as Augustine did in the *City of God* (as the sole necessary form) or the more positive aspect (as the form that fulfills all prior forms). It thus becomes clear that the final form toward which all the religions and philosophies progress in thought are human. Because they are rooted in the creature's natural relationship to God and thus reflect something of this relationship in a variety of ways, some more clearly than others, they may give a hint of certain features

of the ultimate Christian form. But a greater dis-
similitude cuts right through these similarities and
appears in the action of the living God, who died
on the Cross and was raised again.

To be sure, in the natural *religio* and *pietas* toward
God, we see virtues like those of the Asiatic and
Hellenistic traditions: the mastery and tempering of
the irascible passions (*apatheia*), gentleness and per-
severing patience, an enlightened *sympatheia*, a certain humility in the disregarding of the individual's
laws and interests, the higher wisdom that intuitively
grasps the absolute law, a sense of being sheltered
even in being exposed to fate. The highest sphere
gives order to the complex life of the community,
the family, and the individual; the doctrine of the
four cardinal virtues—the "prudence" that risks and
discriminates, the "fortitude" that vanquishes in con-
fidence, the modest hierarchical ordering ("temper-
ance"), and the "justice" that strives for cosmic reason and providence—do not need to be violated
by Christianity, but rather elevated and thereby perfected. But they must be perfected in such a way
that all four dimensions of virtue, and the higher
modes of the God-relationship along with them, are
measured by a standard of judgment that lies beyond what can be achieved or even understood on
the basis of the virtues themselves, and so which
must appear "foolish". When they are so judged,
their deepest meaning must first become meaningless in order to receive a superabundance of mean-

ing in faith, beyond what philosophy can see. It is "wisdom" that drives a person into a Buddhist monastery, who seeks to achieve it in fact by giving away all his earthly goods; but the Christian does not choose the externally analogous path "in order to perfect himself" or even "to find happiness", but because he loves love, the love that was manifest to him in Christ. And it is only within this love that he can come to believe that his self-sacrifice, his casting himself into the sacrifice of the Cross, can have a "meaning" for humanity and for God. Scripture's commandment to turn the other cheek does not contain a primarily ethical meaning—to overcome oneself, or to give the other an example of one's self-mastery or enlightenment—but the meaning of love, which "demands that one suffer humiliation with the humiliated Christ rather than receive honor, to be seen as a fool and madman for Christ's sake, who himself was seen primarily as such, rather than to be esteemed as wise and clever in this world" (Ignatius of Loyola).

Natural virtue is always measured by the greater standard of what is meaningful, of what accords with reason; and this is also necessarily in the acting self's own interest, since he is a part of the comprehensive cosmic order (*ordo universi*). Within the cosmic order, the only foundation for love is the natural harmony of all the parts of the cosmos; the only foundation is being, working, experiencing, and suffering with one another (sym-pathy), being pervaded by a single, common, cosmic breath (sym-pnoia), and thus a higher equilibrium of the standpoints of the I and Thou, the I and the community, and the I and the totality. But the moment an absolute law of (trinitarian) love irrupts like a lightning bolt from the totality, as from the living God, all of these subtle practices of harmony find themselves disrupted, because they are robbed of their claim to centrality, and they are required to order themselves to a point that lies outside of them, a point that, from this moment on, will be the sole form-giving center. The presence of this claim in the post-Christian world makes a return to the ancient harmony between the cosmic and the supra-cosmic impossible. Henceforward, "whoever is not for me, is against me" (Mt 12:30).

But it is equally impossible to expect something like a new cosmic harmony from New Testament love. The principle, as we have repeatedly shown, cannot be reduced to man as a governing center. God remains the center, and man is drawn beyond himself toward the absolute as it manifests itself. He "possesses" love only insofar as love possesses him, which means that he never possesses love in such a way that he could describe it as one of his powers, which lies at his own disposal. To be sure, this does not mean that love remains external to him, but if it does not, it is only because *love* itself takes possession of *him* in his innermost heart—*interius intimo meo*.

Love "organizes" him, not the other way around; it makes man, who puts up constant resistance, into its own instrument. If he ever becomes acquainted with love, he will be careful not to say that he has it. He will at most dare to repeat John's word, as the Church as Bride herself does: "We know that we have passed out of death into life, because we love the brethren" (1 Jn 3:14).

Christians who are sent into the world are put on the path with authority and with the powers to convince, but these powers do not refer to the ones sent; they refer only to the Lord who is proclaimed. The same can be said in relation to faith, hope, and love, insofar as they are meant to draw people's attention to God's form in the world. "We do not come to proclaim ourselves, but Jesus Christ, as Master, while we ourselves [in our eyes] are your servants for Jesus' sake." Therefore this principle cannot become a fixed and easily graspable form that converges with the performance of worldly work. Instead, as a "fragrance of Christ" that blows here and there and back again, beyond all grasp, it must announce something of the infinity of love, "to one a fragrance from death to death, to the other a fragrance from life to life" (2 Cor 2:16). Only a fragrance, but one that compels a decision and lays bare the decision hidden in the depths. Only in this form is there a world culture after Christ.

The form of Christian love, as it appears in the

sign of Christ, is absolutely indivisible. There can be no question at all of certain Christians specializing in the transcendent aspect (the so-called "eschatological" or contemplative aspect) while other Christians specialize in the immanent aspect (as active and "turned toward the world"). To propose something of this sort would be to tear Christ in two and to render his image unintelligible in both directions. There is only one form of *agapē*, which is lived in its wholeness either according to the laws of marriage or according to the laws of the Christian renunciation of marriage, this latter understood as a more explicit call from Christ to a more explicit (and therefore more expressive) following of him. In the state of marriage, the form of *agapē* is impressed upon that of sexual *eros* (and in the familial order, the form is likewise impressed upon the possession of goods, as well as upon the free disposal over them and responsible decision concerning them). In the "state of the counsels", which was Christ's form of life, one's existence takes its form immediately from the original form [*Ur-Form*] of the *agapē* between the Bridegroom, Christ, and his Bride, the Church, in the nuptial bond of the Cross, which is at the same time characterized essentially by the poverty of the Cross and the obedience of the Cross.

Thus, there are not in fact three counsels, but only the counsel to *one* form of life. Accordingly, there are not three vows but only the one consecration of oneself into the crucified form of love as a

single, all-encompassing form of life. All Christians
are inscribed into this form of life through baptism
(Rom 6:3f.), but in the particular form that is "coun-
seled", the form of Christ—as *"forma servi"* [form
of a slave] (Phil 2:7; cf. Mt 20:27–28)—becomes the
fruitful and formative *"forma gregis"* [an example to
the flock] (1 Pet 5:3) and *"forma omnibus credentibus"*
[an example to all believers] (1 Thess 1:7); it becomes a form that represents the form of Christ for
the Church and for the world, and thus, as love that
serves and ministers, it becomes the yeast that disappears into both. For the formative power of Christ
lies in the formlessness of the grain of wheat that
dies and wastes away [*ver-wesen*] in the humus, the
grain that rises again, not in its own form but in that
of the stalk of wheat (Jn 12:24; 1 Cor 15:36, 42–
44).

This movement into the earth (*humilis*) is univer-
sally Christian; with varying emphases, this movement belongs equally to the married and to the un-
married, to active and to contemplative Christians.
This movement superabundantly fulfills the Old Testament movement toward the messianic conquering
and infiltration of the world, and even more superabundantly all of the movement of man's cultivation
(*cultura*) of the world according to God's command.
But the Christian grain of wheat possesses a genuine formative fruitfulness only if it does not encap-
sulate itself within a particular form set alongside all
the forms of the world, an illusory form that thus

condemns itself to sterility, but in imitation of the Founder's archetype squanders itself and offers itself up as a particular form—without being afraid of the dread [*Angst vor der Angst*] of being abandoned and of letting go of oneself. Indeed, for the world, love alone is credible.

10. Love as the Light of the World

Christian love is not the word—not even the ultimate word—that the world says about itself; rather,
it is God's final word about himself and therefore
also about the world. The first thing the Cross does
is cross out the world's word by a Wholly-Other
Word, a Word that the world does not want to hear
at any price. For the world wants to live and rise
again before it dies, while the love of Christ wants
to die in order to rise again in the form of God on
the other side of death, indeed, *in* death. This resurrection in death refuses to be assimilated, instrumen-
talized, or taken in tow by the necrophobic life of
the world. This life, however, which wants to live
before it dies, can find no hope in itself (except in
hopeless constructions)[1] to eternalize that which is
timebound. The only hope the world's will to live

[1] The immortality of the soul; but then what becomes of the single man, who consists of body and soul? He dissolves into the living
whole (according to Plotinus, the Stoics, Averroës, the philosophy
of life, and evolution). But then what becomes of the person and
the uniqueness of love? Transmigration of souls (according to Indian
thought, Pythagoras, and anthroposophy): and here both questions
come to an end.

has comes from God's Word in Jesus Christ; but this is a hope that cannot be anticipated, a hope that lies beyond anything that can possibly be constructed on the basis of the world. This solution seems "desperate" to the world-will; because it proposes death to this will, but for that very reason it reveals the world-will itself to be "desperate", insofar as it has no power over death. But God's proposal appears desperate only to the desperate will to live; in itself, it is pure love, which proves itself in death to be stronger than death, and thus to have conquered precisely that against which the world-will struggles in vain.

If the world decides to allow these two forms of desperation to neutralize one another, it discovers that the Word God utters for the world does not remain external to it but inwardly fulfills it. In other words, it brings the unwilling world precisely to the place that it must go: "Truly, truly, I say to you, when you were young, you girded yourself and walked where you would [περιεπάτεῖς]; but when you are old, you will stretch out your hands, and a 'wholly other' will gird you and carry you where you do not wish to go" (Jn 21:18). What is this "other"? Is it immanent death or the Cross? Or is it perhaps the case that the Cross lies behind death, which represents its condition of possibility? Would this then mean that the whole philosophy of finite existence, which constantly runs up against death as a limit, must finally resolve itself to be resolute

toward the Cross against its will, in order to be resolute toward death? To be sure, this cannot mean
that the Cross is a category of worldly being, which,
though hidden and hard to discover, once discovered, serves to open up the meaning of all things; it
cannot mean it is a sort of dialectical law of "eternal death and becoming", a "speculative Good Fri-
day", which gives human reason the power to take
control of even God's Word, to incorporate death
as an intrinsic moment of life and to crucify itself
in endless repetitions in a thesis, antithesis, and synthesis, in order to raise itself, like a phoenix, out of
its own grave. If the Cross becomes a law at man's
disposal, even if it is an elastic sort of law of the
rhythm of life, then it yet remains a law in St. Paul's
sense, and the power of knowledge thus triumphs
over absolute love. This means that God's sovereign
freedom (which could be radically other than it is)
would come under the judgment of human reason
—and therefore be condemned as that which it truly
is, namely, freedom.

The fact that this road is closed off does not
open up the alternative route, according to which
Christianity would abandon all "knowledge" to the
worldly investigations that belong to science and
philosophy, while the encounter with the Word of
God would be kept for "mere faith" (which is something personal, and without rational justification).
For not only is there genuine knowledge in faith
(the gnosis that the New Testament speaks about so

frequently and so urgently), but for the same reason there is also a reflection on worldly being in the
light of the knowledge of faith. It is a reflection on
the "image"- and "likeness"-character of created being in relation to the divine archetype, which conse-
quently brings to light the watermark of divine love
in every single created being and in the totality of nature as a whole. This sign imprinted on nature, however, comes to light only when the sign of absolute
love appears: the light of the Cross makes worldly
being intelligible, it allows the inchoate forms and
ways of love, which otherwise threaten to stray into
trackless thickets, to receive a foundation in their
true transcendent ground. But wherever the relationship between nature and grace is torn asunder in the
sense of the aforementioned dialectical opposition
between "knowledge" and "faith", worldly being
will necessarily fall under the sign of the constant
dominion of "knowledge" and thus science, tech-
nology, and cybernetics will overpower and suffo-
cate the forces of love within the world. The result
will be a world without women, without children,
without reverence for the form of love in poverty
and humility, a world in which everything is viewed
solely in terms of power or profit-margin, in which
everything that is disinterested and gratuitous and
useless is despised, persecuted, and wiped out, and
even art is forced to wear the mask and the features
of technique.

But if we view creation with the eyes of love, then we will understand it, despite all the evidence that seems to point to the absence of love in the world. We will understand the ultimate purpose of creation: not only the purpose of its essence, which we seem to make some sense of through the various intelligible relationships among individual natures, but the purpose of its existence in general, for which no philosophy can otherwise find a sufficient reason. Why in fact *is* there something rather than nothing? The question remains open regardless of whether one affirms or denies the existence of an absolute being. If there is no absolute being, what reason could there be that these finite, ephemeral things exist in the midst of nothing, things that could never add up to the absolute as a whole or evolve into it? But, on the other hand, if there is an absolute being, and if this being is sufficient unto itself, it is almost more mysterious why there should exist something else. Only a philosophy of freedom and love can account for our existence, though not unless it also interprets the essence of finite being in terms of love. In terms of love—and not, in the final analysis, in terms of consciousness, or spirit, or knowledge, or power, or desire, or usefulness. Rather, all of these must be seen as ways toward and presuppositions for the single fulfilling act that comes to light in a superabundant way in the sign of God.

Thus, beyond existence in general and beyond the

composition of essence, a light breaks on the con-
stitution of being itself,[2] insofar as it subsists in no
other way than in the "refusal-to-cling-to-itself", in
the emptying of itself into the finite and concrete,
while finite entities in turn are able to receive and
retain it, as it is in itself, only as that which does not
hold onto itself. Finite beings are thus trained by it
in giving themselves away in love. One's consciousness, one's self-possession and possession of being,
can grow only and precisely to the extent that one
breaks out of being in and for oneself in the act of
communication, in exchange, and in human and cosmic *sympatheia*. It is only the sign of God that places
all the world's values in their true light, because it
is only here that all the limitations of love and all
the objections to it are overcome, all the mysterious depths of self-sacrificing love are preserved and
wrested from the grip of unrestrained knowledge.[3]

---

[2] On this, see Ferdinand Ulrich, *Homo Abyssus* (1961); Gustav Sie-
werth, *Das Sein als Gleichnis Gottes* (1958); and *Das Schicksal der Meta-
physik von Thomas zu Heidegger* (1959).

[3] The sheltering gaze that love casts upon being and essence, and
its insight into the true nature of spousal love and the genuine love
of children in the hearth of the triune fire of the family, its insight
into genuine friendship, and genuine love of country, in the danger
of its exposure and trials, in its fragmentation into hatred, betrayal,
and death, and in its mysterious transfiguration beyond all conceivable success, preserves what we also find sheltered in the golden core
of myths and mythical religions, and what remains present even in
our ostensibly demythologized world. This is a core that can give rise

Above all, man comes to himself only by being addressed; as one who was brought into existence as a creature, he moreover becomes fully himself only by responding. He himself is the language that God uses to speak to him; how could he not understand himself better here than anywhere else? Coming into existence in God's light, he enters into his own clarity, without thereby endangering his nature (in a spiritualistic fashion) or his creaturehood (through pride). Man becomes whole (*heil*) only in God's salvation (*Heil*).[4] The sign of the God who empties himself into humanity, death, and abandonment by God, shows us why God came forth from himself, indeed descended below himself, as creator of the world: it corresponds to his absolute being and essence to reveal himself in his unfathomable and absolutely uncompelled freedom as inexhaustible love. This love is not the absolute Good beyond being, but is the depth and height, the length and breadth of being itself.

---

to new, credible images in every age. Calderon has shown what it can mean when such images are preserved in being taken up into the supreme Christian image.

[4] See also my essay "God speaks as man", in *Verbum Caro* (1960, 73–99); English ed.: *Explorations in Theology*, vol. 1: *The Word Made Flesh* (San Francisco: Ignatius Press, 1989), 69–93, and also the essays "Die Vollendbarkeit des Menschen" and "Die Vollendbarkeit der Geschichte", both published by Benziger (1963). For the former, see *Word and Redemption*, Essays in Theology 2 (Montreal: Palm Publishers, 1965).

It is for precisely this reason that the eternal primacy of the divine word of love veils itself in impotence and thus allows room for the primacy of the beloved: God's love for his children awakens love in their hearts so that God's love itself may become a child, who is born of a mother and himself in turn awakened to a love that is not only divine but also human. God's Word awakens man's response insofar as he himself becomes the response of love, a love that allows the world to take initiative. The circularity cannot be eliminated; it was conceived and set in motion by God alone, who remains forever above the world, and for that very reason abides in the heart of the world. The center lies in the heart; this is why reverence is given to the incarnate heart, and to the head only when it is "all covered with blood and wounds", because then it reveals the heart.

There is therefore a simple conclusion to the controversy over whether eternal beatitude consists in vision or in love; it can consist only in the loving "vision" of love, for what else but love is there to see in God, and how else can it be seen except from within love?[5]

---

[5] As Thomas Aquinas knew quite well, when he based *visio* on *connaturalitas*, this latter was ordered more to the *donum sapientiae* (which presupposes love) than to the *donum scientiae* [cf. Raymond Martin, "Le principe formel de la contemplation surnaturelle", *Revue Thomiste* (October, 1909)].

Recapitulation

Logos, as reason that understands, can λέγειν—by gathering together (*zusammenlesen*) individual things, factual truths and "dogmas"—only if it sorts (*auslesen*) and picks them out (*verlesen*), grouping them around a chosen (*erlesen*) point. For what concerns the revelation of God in Christ, this point must be one and the same in both fundamental theology and in dogmatics.

The point of integration cannot lie in cosmology (or, for the matter, in a religious ontology); if philosophy and theology were in the past closely entangled in one another, the Reformation and the modern age were justified in distinguishing them, even though they were not justified in allowing reason and faith to fall apart from one another as altogether unrelated.

But it is also not possible that the point should lie in anthropology, because man is no measure for God, and man's answer is no measure for the Word that is sent to him.

It can lie only in revelation itself, which comes from God and provides its own integrating center. This center is set too low, however, in the ordinary Catholic understanding, according to which the Magisterium provides a unity sufficient to gather

up the multiplicity of the dogmas to be believed.
But the Magisterium can justify presenting them as
things to be believed only insofar as it was founded
by Christ, who for his part justified himself as the
one sent by the Father. The Church's formal authority, like Christ's, is ultimately credible only as the
manifestation of the majestic glory of divine love.
But this gives it real credibility.

The center is also set too low by the alternative
doctrine we find in orthodox Protestantism. Instead
of office, it designates the Word of Scripture as the
reference point, which bears witness to itself, interprets itself, and demands obedience—the Word in
its unresolvable existential duality of Old and New
Covenants, justice and grace, and law and Gospel.
Though this may be the formal structure of Scripture, Scripture as a whole is nevertheless only a witness to the concrete incarnate God, who interprets
himself in relation to the absolute love of God.

Liberal Protestant theology understood this in a
fundamental way when it expressed Jesus of Nazareth as the pure face of the eternal Father's love beyond the Old Testament's teaching of the Father
who shows two faces, the face of wrath and the face
of love. But it renders innocuous the kenotic figure
of revelation in the Cross and Resurrection, turning
it into a mere "teaching", or even a "metaphor",
instead of interpreting the form in all seriousness as
the dramatic manifestation of the triune love of God
and as God's battle of love for mankind. It is not the

harmlessness of a verbal teaching that snatches the rotting corpse of the sinner out of the sealed three-day-old tomb and revives the flagging courage of the disciples, sending them into the world as witnesses of the Resurrection.

The reference point presented here lies beyond those in the three theologies just described. It comes to light through the gathering up of the *content* of the kerygma in itself, not gropingly and hesitatingly, but clearly and univocally. As we can easily see, it contains in itself the previous reference points, and for this reason—and only for this reason—it shows itself to be the center that stands above any teaching concerning either the world or man. For the "glory" of the self-manifesting love of God does not call into question any formal authority—neither that of the Church's Magisterium nor that of Scripture—but is rather definitively confirmed by this authority and thus provides the foundation for a deeper obedience, in both theory and practice, to that authority. But the "teaching" about the God of love receives its urgency only in this twofold obedience in love, and through this obedience becomes present as the mystery of love that occurs as an event, here and now. By the same token, this glory does not call into question any philosophical image of God, but rather fulfills these fragmentary images in the radiant mystery of love. Moreover, the formal breadth of philosophical perspectives may help prevent the theologian, the exegete, and any believing Christian from fixing their eyes so narrowly on the historical aspect of Christ's revelation, as the thing of ultimate importance, that they neglect the Holy Spirit. Finally, revelation does not deny any of man's natural and supernatural aspirations, nor does it reject in any way the inner fulfillment of the longings of the *cor inquietum*. Nevertheless, through revelation we come to realize that our restless heart understands itself only if it has already seen the love offered to it by the divine heart that breaks for us upon the Cross.

Love does not come to man "from outside" because the human spirit is tied to the senses, but because love exists only between persons, a fact that every philosophy tends to forget. God, who is for us the Wholly-Other, appears only in the place of the other, in the "sacrament of our brother". And it is only *because* he is the Wholly-Other (in relation to the world) that he is at the same time the *Non-Other* (Cusanus: *De Non-aliud*), the one who, in his otherness, transcends even the inner-worldly opposition between this and that being. Only because he is *over* the world is he *in* it. But being *over* it does not deprive him of the right, the power, and the Word, to reveal himself to us as eternal love, to give himself to us and to make himself comprehensible even in his incomprehensibility. *Consideratio rationabiliter comprehendit incomprehensibile esse.*[1]

---

[1] "Reason comprehends rationally that he is incomprehensible", Anselm, *Monologion* 64 (Schmitt I, 75, 11–12).

Index